Stupid Brokers, Stupid Clients

Trigger Warning: Some Readers Might Find Certain Parts Annoying and Objectionable

If This Is You, Stop Reading Now

KING MIDAS

Copyright © 2018 King Midas
All rights reserved
First Edition

PAGE PUBLISHING, INC.
New York, NY

First originally published by Page Publishing, Inc. 2018

ISBN 978-1-64214-434-5 (Paperback)
ISBN 978-1-64214-435-2 (Digital)

Printed in the United States of America

Contents

Introduction		5
I:	Stupid Clients, Stupid Brokers	7
II:	Buying Stocks That Are Only Going to Go Up	11
III:	When Is It a Good Time to Buy Stocks?	14
IV:	War Stories and Other Conundrums	16
V:	The Grim Reapers	20
VI:	Inheritances	29
VII:	Second Mortgages	35
VIII:	How to Make a Small Fortune in the Market	37
IX:	Stupid Brokers and Gurus	39
X:	Having a Game Plan, or Not	42
XI:	Great Scams I Have Known	45
XII:	Let the Good Times Roll	51
XIII:	Sweat Equity and Other Lies	56
XIV:	Many Are Called . . .	60
XV:	. . . And Few Are Chosen	63
XVI:	Having a Blueprint	68
XVII:	Getting Into the Habit	75
XVIII:	Gold	77
XIX:	Investing Strategies	79
XX:	The Emergency Fund	82
XXI:	The 401(k)	83
XXII:	Plan of Attack	86
XXIII:	Regular IRAs and Roth IRAs	87
XXIV:	Getting Your First House	88
XXV:	Children	91

XXVI:	Insurance 93
XXVII:	College Planning 95
XXVIII:	Retirement Planning 98
XXIX:	Stocks, Bonds, and Mutual Funds 100
XXX:	Masters of the Universe 105
XXXI:	The Really Big Guys 106
XXXII:	Estate Taxes 109
XXXIII:	Nuts and Bolts 113
XXXIV:	Time Lines for Becoming a Millionaire 117

Introduction

Trigger warning : some of the following may be disturbing.

You might wonder why this book is titled *Stupid Clients, Stupid Brokers*. The answer is simple: sometimes it seems that on Wall Street, investors really don't want to make money.

I'm not going to talk about those legacy investors who start out with a ton of money and only try to make a large fortune larger, although a relatively high percentage of those people manage to lose most of it over a lifetime. Squandering money is a large part of their life; many articles maintain that fortunes rarely last three generations. The old saying, "Rags to riches to rags in three generations," is really true.

I'm going to talk about those people who basically start from square one, without a huge sum of money. I'm going to speak from personal experience, covering almost forty-five years of experience on Wall Street, and describe how most people don't bother to do the things necessary to make real money. In other words, they're born poor and stay poor.

I will talk about the mistakes these losers make and the mind-set that keeps them from getting rich. This mind-set is most commonly found among stupid clients and stupid brokers.

Then, I will discuss how investing should be done and what pitfalls you must avoid over a lifetime if you're going to be one of the few who really reach the point of being financially well-off and comfortable.

Because each investor defines financial comfort differently, we'll then discuss how you can go about setting your own goals and objectives while you go about drawing up the blueprint that guides the way to your future. This is not easy, but if you are committed to really doing it and have the courage and determination to do it, it can be done. You can do it.

This book outlines all the basics you will need to get "there," wherever "there" may be for you. If you use the tools I provide, over time you will see a great improvement in your finances.

This book will walk you through many examples of common mistakes, using examples from real life, because they are instructive and illustrative of the kind of errors people make when they're dancing to the music of Wall Street.

In order to show you how to avoid these common pitfalls, we're going to take a walk along Wall Street. In order for you to understand the financial markets, you should understand what Wall Street is and how it really works. There are crooks, charlatans, and fast-buck artists. There are people who will shoot you for twenty-five cents and laugh at your stupidity all the way to the bank. There are still the "masters of the universe" who, as the alpha types at the top, will make ungodly amounts of money while secretaries and sales assistants struggle to pay their bills. There are numerous CEOs who will rape, pillage, and burn a company, run it into the ground, and then walk away with golden parachutes. The difference between rhetoric and reality still continues to make me ill. As someone once said, "More money is stolen with a pen and chicanery than with a gun." Furthermore, as the events of the panic of the fall of 2008 have shown, these people are little more than fools who managed to almost destroy the wealth of Wall Street and Main Street.

The history, fables, legends, and customs of the last decades, gentle investor, will demonstrate how treacherous Wall Street can be and how you have to be extremely careful when negotiating the myriad traps and deceptions that you will encounter.

Stupid Clients, Stupid Brokers

vs.
Smart Clients, Smart Brokers
Which are you?

"My broker talked me into buying this stock, and it did nothing but go down. I think she needed the commission," he said.

"I know that the only time I made money," his companion said, "is when I picked the stock myself."

They tapped their wineglasses together and agreed that brokers were generally pretty stupid and probably crooked too, and the only way to make money in the market was to do their own research and tell the broker what to do. Likewise, they concluded that they probably should be using a discount broker. Unfortunately, the media only feeds their delusions.

After the crash of October 1987, there were jokes going around about shooting brokers in order to make a "killing in the market." It really wasn't so funny because some guy in Florida actually shot and killed his broker.

I've been a stockbroker for over forty years. I started back in the days when we had board markers, usually women, who'd take prices of stocks off the broad tape and post them on huge chalkboards so people could see the last trades in a bunch of individual stocks. We didn't have quote machines, computers, or calculators. I actually remember the first time someone brought a hand calculator into the office. It had a button so you could choose two or four decimal places. It was slow, but it was amazing. Magic. I remember when Intel came public. Nobody knew what a microprocessor was, but we all agreed that it must be a cool thing! How many times have I wished that I'd done nothing but buy Intel for my clients!

I've been in the business so long that when I started, the broad tape reporting last trades were so slow and volume was so low that they had to play it twice during the day just to have something going on in order to keep people interested. It was really slow. Now, that amount of daily volume occurs during the first few seconds of trading each day.

Throughout the five decades I've been in the business, I'm still continually amazed at the interesting and incredibly stupid things investors do. I try my best to educate my clients about what they should do, but few are the ones who listen, and fewer are those who actually do it. The clients that have been with me the longest are the wealthiest, and we have grown wealthy together over the years.

In fact, it took me a number of years to realize that I didn't like dealing with stupid clients, and since then, I have fired many of them. I don't have to do business with people who don't listen to me or whom I don't like.

A good broker is scrupulously honest, thoughtful, patient, risk averse, and paranoid about advice given by the so-called experts on Wall Street. A good broker will be suspicious about the "story" stocks and the "investments" that carry a large commission. One of my favorite good brokers always says, "the bigger the pop," meaning the commission, "the bigger the flop."

There are a lot of smart brokers and a lot of stupid brokers out there. There are brokers who are totally honest, but very stupid, and occasionally, you'll find a broker who is dishonest or a so-called rogue broker. Be careful!

Mainstream brokerage firms try their best to hire only qualified individuals, but the fact is that about 65 percent of all trainees who pass the initial qualifying course and get their license will be out of the business in three years. There was a guy in my office who wouldn't even bother to learn the names of new brokers until they had been there over three years, and it began to look like the newbies would likely be around for a while. When I started, I couldn't understand why he did that. After ten years or so, I began to figure it out. There is another broker in my office who keeps a list of people who have come and gone over time. After forty years, there are about 500 names on that list. He refers to it as the "Gonzo List."

What happens to those people? Where do they go? Where did they come from? What happens to their accounts? Their accounts are generally passed around to other brokers, and the bigger accounts go to the bigger brokers.

Most of the time, these folks just disappear into the maw of the employment universe and are seldom heard from again. Some go to other brokerage firms, but they rarely come back to the office where they started because it reminds them that they didn't have what it takes, whatever that is, to make the grade.

I still don't have any idea what it takes to make it in the brokerage business. Over the years, I have interviewed hundreds of applicants, and a lot of them, who I thought would never make it, did just fine. Many that I thought would be stars did not make the cut. A couple of them had certifiable mental problems, and I never could figure out why they were hired in the first place. Others simply couldn't handle the pressure. Still others couldn't stand the rejection in trying to build a new business. Many just didn't have whatever it takes to be, although employed and supported by a major firm, self-directed and self-employed. I don't, even today, have any idea why I made it, except that I was honest, hardworking, and tenacious. I have a broker friend who maintains that we were too stupid to quit. Failure was never an option.

To help you understand your broker as a person, the following points may be instructive. For example, my wife can't understand how I can go to work every day and not have any expectation of making money.

I think it has something to do with a great faith in the American system of free enterprise and a belief that our country will grow, and companies will grow with the economy. Every day is a new day, and

KING MIDAS

you start the day with no money in your pocket. It is the system of free enterprise at its finest. Some days you make no money, and others turn out to be very profitable, and on balance, you and your clients will prosper. As Woody Allen once said, "Showing up is 90% of success."

Buying Stocks That Are Only Going to Go Up

or

The Crystal Ball Theory of Investing

Stupid clients often call their broker and tell her to "watch that stock and call them when the stock is going to go up." "You are at the market every day," they say, "watching the market and you should know when a stock makes a bottom and is going to shoot up." A good broker will patiently explain that if she had a crystal ball, she'd be on a beach in Tahiti and not at her desk in Cumquat, Idaho. A stupid broker will make a note and call the stupid client back in a couple of days and do the business.

And how much does the broker get paid? Let's take the example of a purchase of 100 shares of IBM at $100 a share. That it's a $10,000 trade, and the undiscounted commission is about $115. Well, the brokerage firm takes about 60% of that for processing and overhead, so the broker gets paid about $46 before taxes. After taxes, maybe she'll net $30. That's for tying up $10,000 of capital for what probably will turn out to be several years as most people won't ever sell their IBM. It's a tough way to make a living for the broker because you have to make a lot of trades to make anything more than gas money.

Then, take a look at how much time it took to do that trade! Let's assume that the broker spent thirty minutes with that client. It works out to about $60 an hour. You can't do enough trades like that to make a living. You don't have enough clients who do that much business. Furthermore, in today's environment, the client will and should demand a discount, and most brokerage firms don't pay the broker anything if the gross commission is less than $85. So it's entirely possible the broker will walk away with nothing. The broker can't afford to spend a lot of time with clients like this. So the broker will naturally gravitate to larger and larger clients who control bigger pools of money. It takes years to develop such a clientele.

Then, there are the clients that tell their brokers that they're interested in selling XYZ when it goes up. They want to sell the stock, but they don't want to do it today. Tomorrow? Next week? If they need the money, they really should sell it today and run all the way to the bank. A good broker might suggest selling half today and then, before selling the rest, waiting awhile to see if it goes up or maybe down. Being a good broker means that a broker practices his profession as an art form as stockbroking is not a science. Sometimes there is a feeling you get that indicates the market might go one way or the other, and once in a while, there are trends that seem to develop, and barring any major surprises, the trend continues. I like to tell people that "if the train is going the right direction, stay on the train."

Many clients like to think it's always the broker's fault when he recommends selling a stock and then it "shoots up." "He just wanted the commission," says the client. "He knew it was going up." Duh! If the stock goes down and the broker recommended hanging on to it, "the broker should have known it was going to go down." The client has put the broker in an impossible, no-win situation.

A good broker will always remind the client of Tahiti and his crystal ball.

Just remember, "Your broker's crystal ball is just as good as yours."

"Why don't you call me more often?" ask many clients. "Simple," I say, "the phone works both ways." What I'm really trying to tell them is that they have some responsibility for their own account, and I can't afford to waste my time. What you can learn from this is that you should build a relationship with your broker. Listen to her and take her recommendations if they make sense. A broker's time is valuable, and you shouldn't waste it. If you don't waste it, they'll call you more often. Be proactive. Pick up the phone and call her.

When Is It a Good Time to Buy Stocks?

There are many theories about buying stocks. Let's buy on Mondays because stocks always go up on Monday. Rallies always occur on Fridays before a three-day weekend because the short sellers don't want to have their money in the market over the weekend in case there is good news. Jeremy Siegel points out that if you stay out of the market in September and October, your long-term results will improve by a percent or two. Most people wish they'd been out of the market in September and October 2008.

"The news is so bad, let's not buy now." That's a perfect argument for the procrastinator. Let's examine the evidence, however, to see if these theories hold water.

From the great crash in 1929, dropping the gold standard in 1933, Pearl Harbor in 1941, the postwar recession, the Korean War, the launching of the first artificial satellite Sputnik in 1957, the missile gap, the Bay of Pigs, the Kennedy assassination, the Six-Day War, the Vietnam War, the first Arab oil embargo, the Nixon resignation, the 1987 stock market crash, the First Gulf War, September 11, and the War in Iraq are all excuses to keep you from buying stocks. Had you used all these reasons, you would have missed an eighty-year bull run that saw the Dow go from the equivalent of $1 in 1929 to $12,968 in 2004 and even higher in 2013.

STUPID BROKERS, STUPID CLIENTS

According to the record keeper and number cruncher, Ibbotson (one of the companies that keep track of numbers), during that time, small company stocks returned a compounded average of 12.7% a year while large company stocks yielded 10.4%. Long-term government bonds came in at 5.4% while inflation chugged along at just 3%. In other words, there was no bad time to buy stocks. Even with the debacle of 2008, these results hold.

But what about buying into bad news? Wouldn't it be better to wait awhile?

The answer is a resounding *no*! This following table is extremely instructive:

Bad News	Immediate Drop in S & P	Next 6 Months	Next Year
Korean War	15% in 5 weeks	+31%	+36%
Sputnik	10% in 3 weeks	+8%	+30%
Arab oil embargo	17% in 9 weeks	-1%	-28%
Nixon resignation	19% in 5 weeks	+30%	+27%
Hunt Brothers' Silver Corner	12% in 4 weeks	+26%	+29%
Gulf War	12% in 3 weeks	+11%	+25%
Average	16% in 5 weeks	+15%	+22%

Interesting? Huh? The lesson is, don't let bad news keep you out of the market. Buy into the weakness! Bad news provides you with a great buying opportunity. Don't let bad news scare you. Warren Buffet says, "Buy when the crowd is selling, and sell when the crowd is buying."

Another interesting statistic for people who insist on timing the market is the following: Being out of the market for just a few days over the preceding ten years reduces your profit and the value of your portfolio substantially because you will miss major upside moves of the market. It is impossible to time the market. Stay invested!

War Stories and Other Conundrums

or

How Listening to Finance Experts Makes You Poor

I used to have a client named John, and we worked together for a long time until he died. I'd been in the business a couple of years, and John and I hit it off at once, and since he always called his own shots, I would give him good service as he was fairly active. His game was buying hot stocks.

If Mazda rotary engines were going to revolutionize the auto industry, he'd watch the stock as it went up and up and up until he couldn't stand it any longer. Finally, after a double or triple, he'd call up and buy some. Unfortunately, for John, he usually did this within about 10% of the top, just before the stock started down.

If CB radios were hot and every trucker and gear-jamming car jockey was going to have one, John would watch the stock price of the CB manufacturer go up and up and up. Finally, when the stock was being hyped by every paper and analyst, John would call up and buy some. Then, the stock would head south.

I finally realized that John was a leading indicator. He was always wrong. He had the philosophy of buying high and selling low; only he didn't know it. I started reminding him of how far a stock had gone up and suggested that maybe the big move was over, and it was too late. I might just as well have saved my breath. This is the headline theory of stock buying—when a stock makes the headlines, rather than buy it, you should sell it.

* * *

Stupid clients always buy last year's hot stuff. There are some fabulous examples taken from a well-known magazine designed to make stupid clients and stupid brokers even stupider. I don't know if they still do it, but every year, they'd publish a list of hot mutual funds to buy for the next twelve months.

For example, in February of 1992, the headline read, "20 Great Mutual Funds to Buy Now."

In February of 1993, it was "the 12 Funds to Buy Now." Only 1 fund is mentioned for two years in a row, so now you own 31 different funds!

In February of 1994, it said "the Nine Best Funds to Buy Now," and none of the previous 31 funds are mentioned again this year, so you now own 40 mutual funds!

In February 1995, it was "Eight Most Dependable Funds." None of the 40 previously mentioned funds is mentioned again, so you now own 48 different mutual funds!

In December 1995, the magazine said to buy "the one that beats them all." That fund had not been mentioned once in the prior four years! Now you own 49 mutual funds! And drum roll, the result after five years, if you followed the magazine's buy recommendations, you had a cumulative return of -0.75% annualized. If you bought what they said to sell, you would have had an annualized return of 18.2%.

So what does that all mean? It means that there are a lot of people out there making lots of money telling stupid clients what to buy and how to do it. And that all boils down to, "If they knew what they were doing, they'd be on the beach in Tahiti." Unfortunately, stupid clients and stupid brokers mostly believe the stupid people in the media. The old saying is true once again, "Those who can, do. Those who can't, teach or maybe write financial columns."

I love to watch the reporters when the market makes a major move, up or down. The words, "shot up," "tanked," and "seriously hurt," and other phrases form a part of sensationalist vocabularies. I love that CNBC, or as we in the business call it, "MTV with ties," now usually reports price movements in percentages. "XYZ shot up 2% in late trading!" Sounds really exciting until you realize that it was really only a $0.25 move on a $12 stock. That's not even enough to cover the commission at a discounter.

When I was cutting my teeth in the brokerage business so long ago, the old-timers told me to beware of brokers and others who were quoting things in percentage moves. It's almost misleading to talk about percentages over short periods. In order to have viewers, the media must sensationalize and hype events in the market. If you listen carefully, most of these reporters know almost nothing about money, wealth, how it works, or how you get it. Most of the others are nearly clueless and thrive on trashing brokers and full-service houses, and they love to tout no-load funds and do-it-yourself plans. These folks just create more losers. In the old days, before the twenty-four-hour media cycle, we used to say that when the headlines were screaming one thing, it was time to do the opposite. In fairness, in times of crisis, CNBC, Bloomberg, and Fox Business News can be very informative, but like everyone else, they can't call the future. Their one great value, in my opinion, is that they interview good "jungle guides" who can talk about what is really happening in the Wall Street jungle.

Every day back in the old times, they used to print in the *Wall Street Journal*, something called the "odd lot purchases and sales." An odd lot means a trade of less than 100 shares. While they don't do it anymore, it was often instructive because the "herd," or stupid clients who didn't have enough money to buy or sell at least 100 shares or more, were always wrong. And, actually, this was a pretty good indicator because it told you what the "little guy" was doing. When the little guy was buying, you should be selling, and when he was selling, you should be buying.

STUPID BROKERS, STUPID CLIENTS

Just look back over the last century, and you can see that those who followed the crowd almost always lost money. When the market makes the headlines, it's usually time to do the opposite.

People are weird. Stupid clients and their stupid brokers are beguiled by the "story." They'd rather listen to the drumbeat of the illiterate press than to the wisdom of the Warren Buffets, Peter Lynches, Charles Brandeses, and Jeremy Siegels of the world. There are many others who have been around through thick and thin, but stupid clients say things like, "It's too slow to follow their advice. I want to get on the bandwagon and buy something that's going to go up." They're looking for instant gratification, and they're going to be disappointed. They invariably buy the sizzle and not the steak. They'll lose their money sooner or later.

One of my favorite quotations about the market is from Warren Buffet: "Pessimism is the most common cause of low prices. We want to do business in such an environment, not because we like pessimism, but because we like the prices it produces. It's optimism that is the enemy of the rational buyer."

Every investor should have this tattooed on their foreheads. In times of panic and fear, the wealth flows from the timid to the patient.

The Grim Reapers

Optimism and Pessimism

When I broke into the business, everything was new and wonderful, just like most things new and wonderful. I even thought that the old-timers had the "secrets" to getting wealthy. Think for a moment about such things as new loves, new marriages, new puppies, new cars, new affairs, and new jobs. The list goes on. I thought that experience on Wall Street brought with it the wisdom of the ages. I figured that the "old guys knew how to make money, and the analysts had some secret that would make me and my clients a lot of money." Oh! The naiveté of youth!

Shortly after, I started to work as a broker. The market, as it has done several times since, was in the toilet. Standard Oil of California, one of the great companies of all time, had gone down from about $75 a share to $18 while the Dow Jones Industrial Average was going from about 950 points to 550. This means that Standard Oil of California had dropped about 70%, and the general market had gone down about 30%. After Standard Oil had gone down this far, our wonderfully erudite oil analyst came out with a sell recommendation right near the bottom. Well, our good old management hit the roof since Standard Oil of California was a great investment banking client and the source of a lot of revenue and profit for the firm. So Standard Oil's president got on the phone to our president, and the analyst was fired. But that was OK as analysts are somewhat similar to the deck chairs on the *Titanic*; they can be wrong a lot, get moved around a lot, but still land a job somewhere. And that's why, boys and girls, analysts seldom come out with a sell recommendation because it ends up costing their firm millions and them, their jobs. So, gentle reader, most of the time you have to take what the analysts say with a grain of salt.

As for me, it was a good lesson to learn early in my career that analysts put their pants on one leg at a time, just like the rest of us. So do the older brokers. So the astute reader might ask, "Who knows how to make money on Wall Street?" The answer is that, "No one knows for sure!"

So why invest? The answer to that one is that there are many wise and important people who have made lots of money for themselves and their clients on Wall Street. And there are many secrets, some of which I'll share with you as we go along. Even today, after the debacle of 2008–2009, over time, the stock market has averaged a gross return of nearly 10% a year. Since the panic of 2008, the market has more than doubled by 2015.

But first, we have to talk about the grim reapers of Wall Street: optimism and pessimism, fear and greed, the steak and the sizzle, the story and the lie, the rush to judgment and impatience. These are all different sides of the same coin. These are, as Shakespeare says, things that "light the way to dusty death." On Wall Street, they are the things that lead the lambs to the slaughter. Stupid clients will blame their stupid brokers, but most brokers (even smart brokers) can do nothing to stop the larger trends. For example, take the bull market of the '90s. From about 1995 to 2000, the market, with a couple of hiccups, went up. The Internet, the dot-com boom was on. The "next big thing" was just around the corner. People were getting rich and richer. Silicon Valley was changing the way the world worked. Everywhere we kept hearing what I consider to be the most dangerous words on Wall Street: "It's different this time." In fact, when you start hearing those words, run, don't walk, away from the Street. When Cisco stock was at $80 a share, people would call up and demand that we buy stock for them. Now it's been, at this writing, around $20 for what seems like years. You can call people and suggest that now is the time to buy, and they'll run like deer because "it's going to go down forever." Well, it may not go up for a while, and it may go down even further, but wouldn't you rather buy it down here at $18 than at $80?

Things were so crazy that people were talking about how many eyeballs were looking at websites. The market was crazy for about three years during the late '90s. Somebody with a business plan written on the back of a napkin would find some underwriter to take their company public, and the stock would not only double or triple when it went public, but in many cases, it'd go up ten times its original offering price. People were coming out of the woodwork to try to get in on the offerings that would make them rich. I had one guy with whom I hadn't spoken in fifteen years call me up and demand that I get him XYZ stock on the offering. I almost laughed at him, but I explained that if I could get that stock, which was doubtful, I would give it to my clients that had been paying the bills for the last decade and that he should give his own broker a call. That's why it's important to build good relationships with a broker. However, the more important lesson for you is to beware of the stock market when it's going crazy. I forget who said it, but sometimes, "it's a good time to remember that the best way to double your money is to fold the bill over and put it back into your pocket."

But that's the way it works on Wall Street: one hand washes the other. Maybe not fair, but when the good times are rolling, you "dance with them that brought you to the party." In those days, I told people many times to call their broker at the discounters and ask them for stock.

Why, I even had a referral that came in to see me because he needed a broker. Let's call him Dick. He was twenty-eight and on top of the world. He had gone to work for XYZ company as an engineer and had accumulated over $800,000 in its stock. He said he wanted a broker who could net him 25–28% a year by trading stocks. I explained to him that that was an unrealistic expectation. I said that if there were such a broker, I'd do business with him myself. Remember to have realistic expectations of 6–10% a year. Some years, you'll do worse than that, and some years, you'll do better.

STUPID BROKERS, STUPID CLIENTS

I pointed out to him that the market was irrationally exuberant right now, and that the historic returns in the market were only in the realm of 10% a year. I told him that, at some point, the averages were likely to revert to the mean. That meant that the market would have to go down enough to take the long-term average back to about 10%. I also told him that he should sell a bunch of his stock and take at least half of it off the table and put it into some conservative securities. He laughed and said that I wasn't the broker for him and that he thought that he could probably do it himself, and that furthermore, his XYZ was going to go up still further. Well, to make a long story longer, he didn't sell even a single share of stock, and now his $800,000 is worth about $12,000. In the final analysis, Dick was a Dick because he didn't know Dick.

A story of greed at its best.

The old Wall Street fable goes like this: bulls make money, bears make money, and pigs get slaughtered. (Bulls think the market will go up and make money. Bears think the market will go down and make money. Pigs try to make too much money and wind up being greedy and getting slaughtered.) Sometimes, you have to take money off the table.

* * *

There are many clients who didn't fall into the stupid-client category like the Dick above. One of the hardest, but one of the best, problems on Wall Street is trying to figure out when to sell off a large amount of appreciated stock and take your profits off the table. In other words, your greed says to hold on because it might go higher, and your fear is that if you do, and you're wrong, you're going to see your money go away. I think the right question to ask is, If you sold all, or most of your stock right now, would the rest of your life work?

At the height of the bull market in 1999 and 2000, I'd tell clients that I couldn't know if their stock would be $20 a share higher or lower next week, but if we took money off the table right now and bought other safer, income-producing securities, would they be OK for the rest of their lives? If the answer was yes, then it was time to take your money out of the stock market. Of the many clients with whom I talked during this period, many did and were happy. Many didn't and were sorry. On Wall Street, "Many are called, and few are chosen." A further complicating factor is the question of taxation. If you have held a stock for more than a year, your profits are taxed away, depending on the largesse of the federal and state governments, at anywhere from 20 to 40%. In other words, if you sell, you are going to have to pay taxes on your gains. If you have held your stock for less than a year, your gains are taxed away at regular income tax rates. We'll discuss taxes and the philosophy of taxes later on in the book.

A good question I've often asked myself is, why are people so stupid when it comes to the stock market? I'm not sure I have a great answer to that question, but I've heard several interesting theories.

First, there is the self-flagellation theory. This one goes something like the "I am not worthy" mantra. There is a huge disconnect between what people think they want and what they think they should legitimately have. It's as if there were a little voice that says that they are not worthy of getting rich. Therefore, they don't get rich because they don't do the things that are necessary to do it. They don't listen to good advice but would rather do stupid things that are practically guaranteed to keep them poor. I think it has something to do with the prophecy that it'd be easier for a camel to pass through the eye of a needle than for a rich man to get into the kingdom of heaven.

Second, there is the lack of discipline. A lot of people think that time, patience, and perseverance are stupid. I love the ads for some of the big independent brokerages where they stress how you can do your own research and trade for nothing. Based on my experience, I think trading is for dummies. Remember, Trading Is Stupid! Most brokers are happy to take money from traders because that is the only person who is going to make money when a client is a "trader." I guess that being a "trader" is like being a "player." That's how you feel active and alive. It's like shooting dice at the casino. There's action.

Some of the people on the TV ads say that they're never called by their broker. Well, communication with your broker, as we've discussed, is a two-way street, and most phones work both ways. Most of the time though, it's not worth a broker's time to call a client who complains that they never hear from their broker and never does anything. If I call a client three times and make three sensible recommendations, and the person doesn't respond favorably, I don't continue to waste my breath. I never pressure a client, but I expect some sort of dialogue and some sort of business, and I refuse to waste my time, which for the last couple of decades is worth about four figures an hour.

Third, it seems that everyone in the market wants a fast buck. "Give me a hot tip!" people say. Hell, if I had a hot tip, I'd keep it to myself, and besides, it'd be illegal to pass it along. If there's a fast buck in the market, you are a very lucky person. People buy real estate for the long term and delude themselves into projecting and being satisfied with all kinds of values. "Hey, I bought this house last week, and it's already appreciated 50%!" they say. "Why, the house down the street just got listed for $X, and I'm making money hand over fist!" It's the fast-buck theory in practice. Let's go buy a lottery ticket.

Fourth, it's the power of the crowd that moves people and markets. Speculators always seem to jump in with both feet at the wrong times. As I mentioned before, it's the "buy high and sell low" theory of investing. Many studies have proven this. Somebody, maybe Morningstar, did a study that showed the fifteen-year return on a major mutual fund was about 15% a year. Then, they did a time-weighted study of individual investors and discovered that the average investor in that fund received a compound annual return of less than 6%. Amazing, you say. Yes, but true. People buy when the market is high and everything looks positive, and then they fearfully sell when things look like crap and the market is low. Just the opposite of what they should really do. Remember, fear and greed. Don't follow the crowd.

They also fail to take into account taxes. If you do the math, and almost nobody does, trading in a taxable account is a loser's game. If you're right, trading makes money for nobody but the broker and the government. If you're wrong, you make money for the broker. But the worst part is that the client, in his haste, loses the chance to make really big bucks. Forgotten is the big fallacy: trading means you have to be right too many times, and you'll miss the big moves in the market. Is Buffet a trader?

There is a fascinating story in Robert G. Hagstrom Jr.'s wonderful book, *The Warren Buffett Way,* which describes the effect of trading when you take into account taxes on an investment versus a buy-and-hold strategy. It goes something like this: "Buffett asks us to imagine what happens if we make a $1 investment that doubles in price each year. If we sell the investment at the end of the first year, we would have a net gain of $0.66 (assuming we're in a 34% tax bracket). If the investment continues to double each year, and we continue to sell, pay the tax, and reinvest the proceeds, at the end of twenty years, we would gain $25,200 after paying taxes of $13,000. If, on the other hand, we purchased a $1 investment that doubled each year and didn't sell until the end of twenty years, we would gain $692,000 after paying taxes of approximately $356,000."

There's an old saying on Wall Street, probably invented by stupid brokers for stupid clients, which says you should never allow tax consequences to influence a decision to buy or sell a stock. Well, I think that philosophy is wrong, and it's just another reason why people don't make money in the market.

Fifth is the investor's IQ. Everybody thinks they're smarter than the market. Well, I'm here to tell you that the market is the great equalizer. Nobody is smarter than the market. Some people may have a run of good luck by thinking they can outsmart it or that they have a system to determine how they should trade. Yet in the long run, and in the long run, don't forget that we're all dead. They blow themselves up. A stupid broker will blow up his/her book, meaning they'll lose their clients by trying to trade it. Once again, the wise elders of the tribe encourage us to buy businesses, not stocks. People will always confuse a bull market with their own intelligence. Remember, a rising tide raises all boats.

An amazing thing is that almost nobody studies the great masters of the market. If you want to be a great artist, you study the great artists. If you want to be a great doctor, you study with great doctors. If you want to be a great anything, you study with the masters of what you want to be. So why don't people study Lynch, Buffett, Fisher, Siegel, Brandes, and all the other elders of the tribe, instead of the local rumor mill or all the pundits that, if they really knew what they were doing, wouldn't be touting stocks. Spend some time reading what the really smart and successful people have to say.

Another thing that I love about stupid clients is how readily they buy stories from some bucket-shop dude calling from New York, or some other faraway place, who is touting penny stocks. A bucket shop is a place that tries to make a profit by selling junk to people. I guess some people figure that the wolf of Wall Street is someone who has an edge and that they can't lose much money on a penny stock because it's only worth pennies. Well, penny stocks can only go down 100%. The truth of the matter is that once a stock gets below about $2 a share, it rarely ever recovers. Unfortunately, usually, if a smart broker tries to get this stupid client to buy something substantial, like a good bank stock or growth stock, the client won't budge.

And, oh, the stories. Buy gold because the world is going to end! It doesn't matter that gold already has gone up 50–100%, and the touters need the suckers to buy so they can sell. Remember 1982, or thereabouts, when gold was about $800 an ounce? There were books on the best seller lists about how gold was going to the moon, and stupid clients threw their money at gold. They'd buy the books from the doomsayers. They'd go to seminars. They'd eventually lose their ass and then wonder what happened. And the stupidity is not limited to just the stupid clients who are rubes. If you don't remember what happened after gold hit $800, I'll remind you. Inflation was controlled, and the price of gold dropped to $250 or so and stayed there for about twenty years. Over the last ten years or so, gold has entered a new bull market, and we've seen it go from its lows to new highs of about $1,700 an ounce and then drop to about $1,200. Once again, the airwaves are full of companies trying to offload their gold at exorbitant prices. Ask yourself, if gold is such a good deal today, why are these guys trying to sell it off? After the drop, a lot of the metals firms have switched to trying to sell silver.

Sometimes, a client will get a call out of the blue. Some bucket-shop dude broker is trying to sell cheap stocks out of inventory.

They'll tell the client that the stock is really moving, and they've got to get in. They'll mark the junk up and then pull the string. It dies, and their phones are disconnected, and they move on. Once again, I sound the alarm: you have to be careful.

Another trick used by the bucket shop is to tell half of their clients to buy a stock and the other half to sell it. The stock will move one way or the other. Then, they'll call the half for whom the trade would have worked and tell them how smart they are. They'll do the same thing over and over until they run out of clients. Half of their list will always think they are the smartest brokers alive; the other half is out of business.

Remember the Hunt brothers in Texas when they tried to corner the silver market? What'd they lose? About two billion dollars. Remember, they were supposed to be the smartest guys in the room.

I fail to understand why people go for the get-rich-quick scheme. But as P. T. Barnum always said, "There's a sucker born every minute." Greed overcomes their fear.

Inheritances

There is an old saying, Greek, I think, that says, "You never know a person until you try to divide an inheritance with him."

First, let's discuss paperwork. Paperwork sounds incredibly boring, but it is incredibly important. When a person sets up an IRA account, a person has to designate a beneficiary—that's the person who gets the money if the person dies. For example, I had a client named Sam who was a great guy and died an untimely death. Anyhow, Sam had gone through an absolutely horrible divorce, and his ex was the ex from hell. The divorce went on for what seemed an eternity, and after the divorce was final, Sam moved to another state, fell in love, and remarried. I sent him the papers necessary for him to sign in order to change the name of the person who would inherit his IRA if he happened to pass on. When Sam opened his IRA, he was happily married to wife number 1 and designated her as the beneficiary. One day, several months later, I was talking to him and said that I didn't remember seeing the papers being returned. He said that he thought he lost them, and would I send another? I told him that it was important to send the papers back, just in case he got on the wrong plane. He certainly didn't want his wife number 1 to get his $500,000 IRA. Well, you can guess what happened.

He didn't get the papers back and died from a sudden heart attack. The new wife wanted the money in Sam's IRA, but the law is clear. The IRA form on file trumps any other documents that a family might have. It doesn't matter what the decedent's trust or will has to say. IRAs, annuities, and other certain types of investments pass to the surviving beneficiary without probate and outside of any formal documents.

Returning to Sam, the ex-wife from hell got all the money. She must have laughed all the way to the bank. The new wife didn't get a dime. And guess who was caught in the middle? Yes, I had to negotiate this political minefield with representatives from both sides. The new wife threatened to sue me and my firm, but the law was clear. I had tried repeatedly, but the beneficiary had not been changed, so she got nothing. I felt sorry for her, but my hands were tied. Remember, paperwork is important.

Stupid clients are rarely advised by stupid brokers to get their paperwork in order. Most stupid brokers don't even do it for themselves. Even when stupid clients are advised by smart brokers to get their estate planning docs in order, they rarely do it because they don't like to contemplate their own mortality. I've bugged clients, sometimes for years, before they got around to it. If you have an estate attorney, and you should, please follow her directions: Get your paperwork in, and make sure all your accounts are properly titled. A good estate attorney will bother you periodically until she has copies of all the accounts and beneficiaries.

Then, there are the clients who think they can do their estate planning on their own. If you have any substantial money in your possession, you need a professional to get your paperwork in order.

Let's talk a moment about "trust mills." It seems like every mobile-home park in the world has someone who can put together a living trust on the cheap. Usually, but not always, mobile-home park residents don't have a lot of money, and I've seen many problems arise from these inexpensive boilerplate trusts. These people who populate the "trust mills" rarely follow up to properly finish the job. When a trust is written, a good attorney will follow up and make sure that all your property, including brokerage accounts, homes, other real estate and beneficiary forms, are properly titled. Even if you have a living trust, it doesn't matter if you don't have your other accounts titled correctly. Always, in this case, the Joint Tenants with right of Survivorship trumps the trust so titling of accounts is really important. Stupid clients and their stupid brokers don't have a clue about negotiating even the most simple of minefields. A good broker will have a stable of experts that he can refer clients to in order to get them the best help they can get. Remember, if you have any real money at all, you should pay for the best advice you can get. A living trust also avoids the problems inherent in probating an estate. If you happen to own property that's out of your state, you have to open an ancillary probate, which can get really messy and expensive.

If I get passionate about living trusts, I really get passionate about estate taxes. In fact I think estate taxes are immoral As we go to press, Congress is debating, again, the amount of money that can pass to heirs free of estate tax, or as it is sometimes called, the death tax. I've never liked double taxation in any form, whether in dividends or estate taxes. It is just one more way that the government thinks that it is more deserving of your money than your own family. Anyway, people who think they have an estate tax problem should consider a living trust. The more money you have and the more complicated your situation is, the more you should expect to pay a good attorney for writing a good trust.

If you don't have a trust and have just a simple will, you know the kind: "I die, Mom gets it. She dies, I get it." If this is all you have, it's certainly better than not having one at all, but it is far from perfect. Remember, if you don't plan your estate, your friendly state government has a plan for you, and it probably is nothing you'd like. Sometimes, even someone you really hate will get the money. Furthermore, probate and administrative fees will take a lot of your money before the state-designated people inherit it.

With your simple will, not much happens when the first person dies as most property passes to the survivor with no tax. But at the second death, and here we're talking about married couples, only (at this writing) a certain amount will pass to your heirs without estate tax. With a properly written trust, double the exempted amount will pass to your heirs without any tax. This will save your heirs a lot of money in estate taxes. Furthermore, with just a simple will, some lawyer will take, depending on where you live, about 5% just for the pleasure of probating your estate. Sometimes, the executor will take another 5%. With a simple will, the settlement process has to go through the court system. This can not only take a large amount of time, but it is very expensive. With a trust, these costs are usually avoided. No attorney will take an executor's fee, although if your estate is complicated, they make take a fee to make sure the estate is properly settled, and your final wishes are carried out. Another benefit of a trust is that it can be settled quickly, without publicity, and your beneficiaries will get what's due them sooner rather than later.

One day when I was talking to my father, for whom a good trust had been written by an excellent attorney, I said that I was pleased that he had done that. He said that he didn't have a trust any longer as another attorney had said that he didn't need one, and that all he needed was a simple will. I almost fell off my chair and immediately called an attorney in my stable of experts, and we went down the same day, as my dad was dying of cancer at that time and had a new trust written. When my dad died, and the notice appeared in the paper, I got a call from the first attorney who asked me if he could help "settle" my dad's estate. I said, "No, thanks, as our new trust didn't need any help." Dishonest, unethical attorneys have stolen more money with a pen than with a gun. Well, I was glad I asked my dad the question as the trust saved a significant amount of money for my mom and for my sister and me. Get a living trust and get a good one.

Another sad example is one from one of my favorite clients. When he retired from a large international corporation at age sixty-two, he didn't bother to consult me when he took out his pension. He chose to take out a pension based on his single life expectancy only. When a person does this, he gets more money each month than with other options for life, but that is exactly what it means, for life. When he dies, the spouse, or other survivor, gets nothing. In any case, Dave and his wife were going to live large on his pension and pass many happy years before riding off to that big stock market in the sky. Well, Dave lived for five months after retiring and died suddenly from a massive heart attack. The first I knew about this was when his wife called me and told me that the pension was gone. I said I thought it was gone for good, but that we should consult an attorney. She did, and they tried to get the corporation to continue the pension, but once again, the law is clear, and the decision for "life only" was irrevocable. In those days, a spouse didn't have to sign off on the option. Today, thankfully, it's different, but you still have to be careful. A spouse has to sign off on the option chosen. Usually, it's best to take a smaller amount just in case.

A smart broker is a treasure trove of information and good advice. Sometimes a good broker's worth is measured in things other than whether or not a stock goes up. A good broker will have an arsenal of tools to help a client negotiate the minefields of financial planning and wealth creation.

Then, there are the family members that don't speak to each other because the now-deceased parents left more money to one beneficiary rather than the other.

"You tricked Mom into giving you the house because you lived with her and took care of her."

"Mom liked me better, and you must have suckered her when she was sick."

I've seen families that are torn apart by inheritances, and blood feuds start because someone felt cheated by an inheritance, or they thought someone took something that should have gone to someone else. Here is where a good trust can solve problems. Sometimes, a good attorney will have the person writing the trust do a videotape to show that the client is in good shape and is not acting under duress. This avoids charges that the client is being overly and unduly influenced by individuals or other family members.

Then, there are the "good for nothing" kids that keep after Mom and Dad for money. Kids in their thirties and forties that haven't been able to hold a steady job in their lives go to their parents and practically demand money because they need a new car, a new suit, or some money to make their latest get-rich-quick scheme work.

"Mom, I just need $25,000 to get this project off the ground, and I'll never bother you again."

I can't tell you how many calls I've fielded over the years. I had one client call me and ask me if he should give his forty-five-year old son $30,000 for the company Junior was starting. The son was being persistent, obnoxious, and demanding. Worse still was the fact that the man's wife, the kid's mother, was literally dying from breast cancer. I, like a good broker should, told him that he couldn't afford it and shouldn't give the kid the money. I told him to blame the decision on me to take some of the heat off him.

A good broker gets involved with good clients and their lives. To be able to give good financial and planning advice, a good broker sometimes becomes part of a family. The New York Stock Exchange has a rule, rule 405, which says a broker must "know your customer." It's good advice. If your broker doesn't take the time to get to know you, find another broker.

Second Mortgages

Second mortgages, how sweet the sound! If I had a nickel for every time I heard those words from stupid clients and even once in a while from smart clients, I'd be a wealthy man. Their big attraction is that they pay a higher rate of return, generally 5–7% higher than a first mortgage. That's the attraction. The downside is that if the property owner defaults, the holder of the first mortgage has first claim on the property. If you can't step up and pay off the first mortgage, you'll generally wind up with nothing.

"Oh, but I have a good real estate broker who carefully evaluates each property before he asks me to invest." Well, just ask folks after the real estate debacle of 2008–2012.

The story of two clients should suffice. One, an astute and careful man, had a complete portfolio of several hundred thousand dollars when he came to me, and we decided that because he was risk averse and nearing retirement, we'd try to remove his seconds from his portfolio as they matured. We were nearing the end of this program when a note defaulted, and he lost the value of the note. He told me that he wished he'd never heard of seconds. With this one event, he'd lost the entire profit—read higher interest received—from several years of investing.

Another involves a young widow who invested several hundred thousand dollars in her new boy toy's real estate venture. I don't think this investment lasted six months before the owner of the property, who now had her money, went broke and took her money. She couldn't afford it.

At least the first investor could afford the loss.

After the real estate disaster of the last decade, even the holders of first mortgages lost a lot of their money as real estate prices declined, declined, and declined.

How to Make a Small Fortune in the Market

The old saying goes, "If you want to make a small fortune in the market, start with a big one." Unfortunately, for many people, this is true. I know I've said it before, and I know I'll say it again. You have to be careful! Wall Street is a jungle, and like being in any jungle, you need a jungle guide. Yes, some people can do it on their own, but most people don't have the time, energy, or expertise to do it themselves. You need an experienced person to guide you. She is well worth the money you're paying her.

One of my richest clients says that he doesn't mind paying taxes because that means he's making money. He also doesn't mind paying commissions or fees because that means he'll always get the best advice and service that I can provide as quickly as I can provide it.

A lot of people will go to their banker or a low-cost broker for advice. Quite simply, and maybe a bit unfairly, they'll be talking to people who can't make it on their own and who are not good enough to attract a clientele that will sustain them. You'll remember that there are a lot of brokers in good firms who can't make it either, so I'll tell you a secret. If you are looking for an advisor, you should walk in to an office and ask to see the branch manager who will try to put you together with an experienced broker who should be compatible with you. Tell him or her what you're looking for. If you go in and just ask for a broker, you'll probably wind up with the newest rookie in the office who is probably not the type of broker you're looking for. Tell the manager you want a broker with at least ten years of experience and who is a senior member of the firm; in other words, someone who has been around for a while.

Working together, you'll do a heck a lot better than you ever would trying to do it yourself. I just love the advertisements on television that imply that you can do just fine by using the "tools that the pros use." Well, yes, they do have some fancy software that sometimes helps them find a cool stock or maybe an aid to timing a purchase, but I find it grossly misleading to pretend that Joe Sixpack, living in Cumquat, Idaho, can find the time and energy to trade the market and try to compete against those folks who do it for a living. The proof is simply that the "pros" can't do it with any consistency. That's why there are so many horror stories about traders losing their butts in the market.

That's also why there are so many stupid brokers out there who will never ever be financially secure.

Some of the other things that I'd be very careful about, or avoid entirely, are things like annuities. They have their place, but I'd never do an annuity for a person much over fifty-five. Sometimes, an income annuity is suitable for an older person, but they are heavily stacked in favor of the insurance companies, and sometimes your heirs wind up with nothing.

For long-term money, a variable annuity will shelter you from current taxes, but taxes will be due when you start to withdraw money from it. If you are under 59½, you are not only socked for current income taxes, but you get a 10% tax penalty, so you wind up losing almost 50% of your profits.

Stupid Brokers and Gurus

Long-Term Capital Management
Pension Guarantees
and
Other Nobel Prize Winners and Assorted Idiots

"If you're so smart, why ain'tcha rich?" How many times have you heard this? I will bet you've heard it and probably said it yourself. There are many smart people on Wall Street, but they're really just like you and me. They put their pants on one leg at a time, just like we do. Yet investors are continually blinded by the aura of flashy computer programs, Nobel Prize winners, graduates of Ivy League universities, and other assorted titled individuals.

Let's examine some recent examples that have strutted across the stage that is the investing world. One of the most glaring examples is that of long-term capital management. This group raised billions of dollars from hundreds of millionaires. As you know, money attracts money, and a lot of people justified their investment by noting that if so many other millionaires are doing it, it must be right.

As usual, there was a polished front man who glibly pointed out that there are several Nobel laureates on the board who are designing software that will be "state of the art" and which will lead to riches beyond their wildest imaginations. The plan was to leverage investments by using derivatives in markets throughout the world. In other words, the value of the original investment would depend on what other securities did. To make a long story short, these geniuses leveraged (borrowed so much money) themselves so much, that at the end, they didn't know what they had. I think that they finally had almost 20 billion dollars in borrowed money outstanding. Finally, the chairman of the Federal Reserve, Alan Greenspan, had to convene a group from Wall Street to put up a huge sum of money to bail the whole thing out because he feared that without an infusion of capital, the whole thing would self-destruct and overwhelm the international financial markets, causing worldwide financial panics. In the long run, the Nobel Prize winners didn't know what they were doing and only led more lambs, albeit rich ones, to the slaughter.

As a further example, the federal government had to bail out Wall Street in the 2008–2009 credit crunch and panic. It's more proof that just because you're rich, you aren't necessarily smart. Wall Street didn't cause the panic, but that's another story.

I've said that you have to be careful, and I mean it. If you don't understand an investment, don't make it. Long-term capital management was trying to do it with smoke and mirrors, and in the final analysis, even these really smart guys didn't understand what they were doing. Their whole program reminds me of chaos theory: you know, if a butterfly flaps its wings in Brazil, it will cause a hurricane to form off the coast of Africa. If you want to read a fascinating book, read the history of long-term capital management.

Examples abound! At this writing, a lot of pension plans are under pressure because they are underfunded. It's totally logical that there are shortfalls in contributions because management isn't stupid. Management knows that if they underfund these pensions, the government will probably be forced to step in and take over the plan, and the taxpayers will bail them out. The poor participants, however, who have banked on the dollars from the pension funds will wind up holding the bag because the government doesn't have to pay out the same amounts that the company had to. Therefore, many people are finding their monthly checks cut by huge percentages. How would you like it if you were receiving $4,000 a month, and then suddenly, you were forced to lower your expectations to only receive $1,300 a month? It's sad but true.

It is just one more reason that you have to take care of yourself. You'd better get serious about building up your own nest egg because if it's yours, it's yours, and unlike a company pension plan, nobody can take it away from you. You can lose it, but they can't take it away from you.

Having a Game Plan, or Not

Another of the amazing things I've seen is the way people approach the road to wealth. It's kind of like a man driving around and not asking for directions. Stupid clients call and will say something like, "My sister's friend works for this company, and they think it's going up. Buy me some." OK, we buy 100, 200, or 300 shares, and that's the end of it. They are one-trade wonders. They rarely follow up the first trade with additional contributions. They don't ask what they're supposed to do to become wealthy. They don't even know why they're spending the money on this stock except that it's supposed to go up because their sister's friend said it will.

I think most people approach the markets with about as much aforethought as they approach most things in life; in other words, with hardly any idea of what they're doing or supposed to do. People usually say that the reason they're investing is that they want to make money. They never stop to wonder how, why, how much, or anything else about what it takes to *really* make *real* money. They have no goals or plans. If a good broker bothers to ask them where they'd like to be in five years from a financial point of view, they don't have a clue.

I usually tell people that there are basically three ways to make money:

1. Inherit it, or in other words, be the beneficiary of the "lucky sperm."

2. Get lucky. You win the lottery, marry very well, or go to work for a successful start-up, and get a bunch of founders' stock.

3. Do it the old-fashioned way: save it and put it to work for yourself over many, many years.

Time, patience, and perseverance are the golden secrets. You should be in the markets for a long time, have the patience to wait out the good and the bad times, have perseverance, and be very intentional about saving and investing your money.

I think it's a crime that money is not taught in schools. Children should be exposed to the simple ways that they can accumulate wealth. I actually think that there is a bias against becoming wealthy. The language is full of phrases like "filthy lucre" and "money is the root of all evil." When somebody says, "It's not about the money," you'd better believe that it's about the money. Others: "A fool and her money are soon parted," "Poor little rich kid," and many more. In today's society, with politicians railing against "rich people" and "the 1%," it's sometimes hard to think about getting rich. It's almost as if it's a sin to be, or want to be, rich.

There are so many poor people because there are so many poor people. Instant gratification seems to be the byword of the day when everyone spends, or overspends, what they make and live far beyond their means. Whatever happened to saving and putting money away for a rainy day? In California, where home values have skyrocketed over the years, I'm often told that a person's house is their best investment. This argument makes me want to pull my hair out. A person's residence is not really an investment; it's a use asset. A use asset is something that you own that doesn't produce much for you except the use you get out of it. It's true that the equity in a house can grow and grow, but there are only a couple of ways that a person can tap that equity: either borrow it out and pay a bank or mortgage company interest to use the money, or cash out of the house and downsize. I suppose that's why so many Californians are moving to Arizona, Nevada, or Oregon. A person's second house is the investment that can create additional real wealth.

But returning to my original point, why don't people approach their investment life as they approach their real life? You don't build a house without a design and blueprints. You don't, unless you're a man, go somewhere without a map. You don't invest in a new venture without a business plan. And you shouldn't embark on a path to accumulate wealth without a good plan. Really, it's kind of simple: you decide how much money you want, how many years you have to get there, how much risk you want to take, and how much money you have to put aside to get there.

I once had a stupid client, Will, who was the son of a smart client, come to me and say that he was now forty-five, and it was time to start putting money away for retirement. He told me that his goal was to have about $2,000,000 when he reached retirement age of sixty-two. We talked awhile, and it turned out that he had saved almost nothing over his first forty-five years. He liked living large and had no money put aside. Well, I crunched some numbers for him and told him that he had to save something like $4,500 a month to get to where he wanted to be. I asked him if he could do that, and he just kind of mumbled and said that he'd think about it. That was the last I ever saw of him. Later on, I'll discuss how much you have to save, at what age, to become a millionaire.

It's trite, but most people don't plan to fail. They fail to plan. Therefore, they don't accumulate any real money and wake up somewhere around age fifty and wonder what the hell they're going to do when they're ten years older and they're too old and can't work anymore.

That's why about two-thirds of the people in the United States retire with a net worth of less than $75,000 and an income of little more than what Social Security pays them each month.

Great Scams I Have Known

"Wall Street is a jungle." There are a lot of animals that instead of eating you will eat your wallet. I believe that the value of a good broker is often to protect clients from the carnivores roaming the canyons of "the Street."

Let's take the Over-the-Counter market. This market has gotten better over the years, but in the old days, this market was run by guys and gals trading nonlisted stocks. What a game! Who knew what the real prices were? You get a lousy execution on a stock and call the trader. Well, you're told, "It was a volatile market, and there were executions all over the place." You, and your client, got screwed, and there wasn't much you could do about it. You could cry and moan, but that and a quarter would get you cup of coffee. The over-the-counter bond market was even worse. Back in the eighties, when Congress, in its wisdom, caused the savings and loan debacle and screwed up all the limited partnerships that had been built on the previous law, bond traders would routinely take advantage of naive S&L securities traders by taking 10 points out of the middle of the trade. In other words, they'd buy securities from these naives for 55 and sell them similar securities for 65. In plain English, they'd pay $550 per $1,000 bond and turn right around and sell them similar stuff for $650. This may not sound like much, but when the S&Ls were trading $50,000,000 of face amount in order to take a tax loss, this was a commission of about $5,000,000. People were making a lot of money, and the rubes didn't even feel the knife as it went in.

Traders are a special breed, and most of them would shoot their grandmother for twenty-five cents. In fairness, not all traders are so ruthless. A good broker soon learns the names of the good ones and the ones who will treat clients fairly.

* * *

One of my favorite stories occurred during my first years in the business. There was a guy named Frank who had a sale/leaseback program involving railroad tank cars. The story was wonderful. You could actually buy your own tank car for $30,000 and lease it back to the railroad. The railroad would pay you monthly rent plus they'd pay you for every mile the car rolled over their track. Since each car had its own unique number painted on the side, you could actually go down to the railroad crossings and watch for your own personal tank car to pass by. Why, you even got a model tank car mounted on track that you could put on your desk. Furthermore, you would get depreciation on the car so that, essentially, the money you made could be sheltered from income tax. And to make it even better, as I recall, your $30,000 provided an investment tax credit. Wow, those cars sold like hot cakes. What a way cool investment!

Well, if it sounded too good to be true, it probably was too good to be true. We sold a bunch of these cars, and after a few weeks, our underwriting department wanted to take delivery of the cars and get them rolling. Frank hemmed and hawed and shuffled around a bit, and our guys finally got suspicious and demanded to see the factory and the rail yard where these cars were made and stored. Geez, it turned out that there were no cars, never were, and the whole thing was a scam. Without flinching, our firm sent out a wire telling us to tell our clients that nobody would lose any money, and that our firm would guarantee that they got their money and expenses back. Furthermore, the brokers got to keep their commissions. That was, and still is, an honest brokerage firm. I think the underwriters that got duped lost their jobs, but went merrily on to other firms where they were readily hired.

A few years later, Frank showed up in the newspapers again with a scam that didn't involve securities, but dealt with nonexistent diamonds. I think he went to the slam for that one.

In the early '80s, limited partnerships were extremely popular. Talk about big money. Wall Street went nuts over these things. They included ranches, oil wells, apartment buildings, shopping centers, windmill farms, general partners, limited partners, and limited liability. These things had it all. There were huge commissions involved on the one side and huge loans on the other. Stupid brokers sold the pants off them, reaped the rewards, and finally, most of them blew up their books; i.e., they lost all their clients' money. Even smart brokers got roped in, but most of them survived because they didn't totally believe all the hype. Remember the crowd theory. When the crowd loves it, run, don't walk, away from it.

Well, in my opinion, what blew all these up was Congress. In the tax reform of 1986, Congress changed the active/passive management rules, and all of a sudden, the limited partnerships that were done previously to 1986 didn't work anymore because all the tax reasons for their existence went away. I still, to this day, do not understand why Congress didn't grandfather in all the old deals until they died a natural death and apply the new rules to new partnerships. So much wealth was wiped out; it was unbelievable. For ten years, people got K-1s from these deals, and every tax time, there were new reasons for people to hate their brokers.

* * *

Then, there is the story of a Nevada Brothel when it wanted to go public. For the uninitiated, the Nevada Brothel was one of the most famous brothels in all of Nevada located just outside of Reno. One author described it as "a candy store full of beautiful women, take your pick." Of course, I've never been there, but there are stories, and I know personally that several brokers took very seriously their obligation to do their due diligence, which means digging deeper into the story, when trying to understand the initial public offering for the Nevada Brothel shares.

It turned out that the Business was in serious financial difficulties, and in order to solve their problems, they wanted to raise money by selling shares to the world so they would be able to use the money to improve and save the business. They never did go public, but I managed to get a preliminary prospectus that described all the Business's operations in great detail. I decided that it'd be worth it to invest a few dollars just to have a stock certificate from the Nevada Brothel that you could hang on the wall. The annual reports would probably be fun too. They described an executive position that seemed to attract a lot of interest, and that was the post of director of independent contractor operations and training. That sounded like the job to have.

Sometime in the 1980s or 1990s, the government seized the Ranch because it failed to pay back taxes. The government, as usual, proved to be so inept that even when selling whiskey and sex, they drove it into bankruptcy. I've heard that the previous owner is alive and well living in South America.

*   *   *

Options don't really fall into the scam category, except that they almost never work. People who buy options are doing little more than gambling. Studies show that between 80 and 85% of all purchased options expire worthless. That means that almost everyone who buys options loses their money. But people still do it. Stupid clients and stupid brokers engage in this type of self-destructive behavior. I refuse to recommend options to anyone and have refused to do the business even when pressed. Some people have done it anyway and have been sorry.

I had a good friend named Harry. He was a great fishing buddy and passed on a couple of years ago. Anyway, he knew a guy who had a system. He said he wanted to follow this system. I told him that no way was I going to help him lose his money. He said that the system worked. He took me to lunch with this guy. He begged and pleaded for a long time. Finally, I said that I'd put the orders in for him but no way was I going to do anything to influence his decisions. He liked the action and traded like a madman for quite some time before he lost all his money and decided that I was right. His buddy also lost all his money. At least I never wavered in my belief. Some people say that I never ever should have even placed the orders for him, but I did anyway.

The only kind of option trading that makes any sense to me at all is option writing. This is when a person owns a stock and sells call options against the long position. This provides income for the investor and is done with very little risk. The only major problem with this type of investing is that it limits the upside on the long position. In other words, it caps the return that an investor can make.

* * *

A smart broker working with smart clients can avoid many of the pitfalls waiting for the unwary. It's impossible to avoid every single problem in investment, but the odds greatly improve when you're working with someone who cares about you and knows the ways of Wall Street. I'll say it again, "It's a jungle out there, and you'd better have a good jungle guide." You'll never find one at the online wire houses. Do jungle guides make mistakes? Sure, but rarely do they let the animals eat them alive.

I will warn again about people who say that they can do it all by themselves. I will rail against all the pundits who say that brokers and planners are unnecessary.

Bull crap! I don't fully understand the motives of these folks except that there must be a huge jealousy factor embedded in their personalities. For some reason, they think that they, secure in their ivory towers, can impartially advise people and point them to the way to wealth. I, on the other hand, believe that most people need a smart broker to guide, cajole, encourage, and push them on the pathway to wealth. In fact, I think a smart broker regards his/her calling as an economic and financial holy mission. Once again, I hear the refrain: "Those who can, do, and those who can't, bloviate and pontificate."

KING MIDAS

* * *

Whenever there are big bucks involved, there are those who try to cut corners. As the old saying goes, "More money has been stolen with a pen than with a gun." Recently, we have had the Bernie Madoff, WorldCom, Enron, Adelphia, and other scandals involving zillions of dollars. Finally, some of these players are going to the slam, but I think it's unfair that these people get away with keeping a lot of their ill-gotten gains. Even if they go to the big house, their families usually get to keep most of the money.

There used to be a guy who wrote the "Heard on the Street" piece in *the Wall Street Journal*. I think his name was Pat. His pen could make or break a stock. We used to wake up in the morning and look at his column to see what stock was going to get trashed that day. It was a very powerful thing and something that we had absolutely no control over. But we, and our clients, would pay the price.

Well, it ultimately turned out that he wasn't making enough money, and as I recall, he was tipping off his buddies who traded on the recommendations that they knew were coming. When the whole plot unraveled, a lot of people paid the price. I don't recall what the final disposition of the matter was, except that he lost his job, but it just goes to show how so many scams are put together and how much risk people are exposed to by unscrupulous players on Wall Street. Let's hear it for the regulators.

I have no patience whatsoever with people who try to rip off the system.

Let the Good Times Roll

Most clients have no clue about what the business is like from the other side of the table. In other words, what's it like to be a broker? Another *trigger* warning.

When I was a rookie broker, I remember an old-timer saying that we were overpaid in the good times and underpaid in the bad. I really didn't know what he was talking about at the time because I hadn't worked through any good times or bad times. In fact, I hadn't even begun working yet.

Being a broker is probably one of the best jobs to have and, at the same time, one of the worst. I have already talked about the washout rate being about 65% after the first three years, but I haven't talked about the pressure that a broker is constantly under. A broker works with the most precious commodity, after their family, which people have: their money. The decisions that a broker makes with his clients are among the most important ones that a client ever makes. Multiply those decisions by dozens a day and thousands a year and compound them all by the fact that the broker has no power to control the price changes that are constantly taking place.

Some of us old guys like to say that every time we pick up the phone, we are opening ourselves up to potential problems. That means that any time we take an order or suggest an order, we are at risk. We are at risk of hearing the order wrong, entering it wrong, having a client renege, or having a client initiate a lawsuit even several years after the fact, if the investment doesn't turn out. It won't even matter who solicited the order, the lawsuit still runs, and brokerage firms spend hundreds of millions of dollars a year defending themselves and their brokers from both serious and frivolous lawsuits. And what is a broker's defense? It usually amounts to writing things down in a Day-Timer, a notebook, which provides a contemporaneous record of what transpires. Unfortunately, most brokers do a terrible job of writing each and every conversation down. Consequently, most brokers who survive in the business become pretty conservative and risk averse.

A friend of mine has a client who has an accent. This good, smart client gave this broker an order to sell 50,000 shares of a forty-dollar stock. This $2,000,000 trade was fairly routine for this client and was nothing out of the ordinary. The broker repeated the order back to the client and called his client back to confirm. The client said "50,000? I said 15,000." The broker said that he'd written down 50,000, and the client, who is totally honest and responsible, said that it was a mistake and must have been his accent. The smart broker first assured the client that he was not at risk and that he'd take care of the error. The procedure for taking care of an error is to call the office manager immediately and tell her what happened. Usually, the manager just takes over and works it out; however, in this case, the broker was lucky. The stock moved down by about 10 cents a share, and the firm, actually the broker's error account, made a profit of about $3,500 (35,000 shares × $0.10). Neither the broker nor the client gets this money, and after a year, unless there are offsetting errors made by the broker, the firm gets the money. Let's take the opposite case. If the stock had continued up another $0.10, the broker would have eaten an error of $3,500. This is a nonnegotiable policy of the firm, and the loss is rarely shared by the firm. The broker has to take it all and has to pay it back to the firm. It comes out net, after tax, and not from pretax gross commission. Fair, no, but them's the rules. (Note: this policy has since been changed, and the broker no longer eats the error.)

STUPID BROKERS, STUPID CLIENTS

* * *

In my old firm, we used to have the illusion of paid vacations. The way this worked was that you could take any vacation you wanted, and supposedly, you got paid for the time off. In reality, if any commissions came in while you were away, you didn't get any of them until you paid for your monthly guarantee. So you really got nothing in the way of a paid vacation. You just got your basic draw, and any commissions that came in went to the firm. After several years of this charade, the firm did away with the illusion of paid vacations for brokers. You just took the time off that you wanted.

At the same time, it is the best business in the world. You get to work in a stimulating environment with intelligent people who are mentally very quick. You get to work with smart clients who are extremely interesting. You get to take as much time off as you want as long as you keep your nose clean and do enough business to be successful. There is no arbitrary ceiling that limits how much money you can make. If you work, you get paid. Unlike the corporate world, you don't have to depend on the whims of some superior to give you a raise once in a while. In my world, subject to the laws and regulations of the business, you are your own boss and responsible for your own business. Basically, although you work for a major firm, you are self-employed. Every day it's always sink or sail.

It's also very hard to survive during the bad times, which happen far too often. And what about the bad times? Try to put yourself in a broker's shoes for a moment. She's done her best and likes her clients, and then a Nixon, oil crisis, stagflation, the great Internet crash of the early 2000s, or the great recession of 2008–9 comes along. The value of her client's portfolios drops 20, 30, or 40%. This is bad, but the worst part is drip, drip, drip as the markets go down for days, then weeks, then months and then years. She hates to go in to work. Clients continually look to her for guidance, and she is really helpless. She says that this too shall pass. The market and the country will recover.

This is the time when you're underpaid. This is why brokers tend to drink, have heart problems and ulcers. They care about their clients and can't control what's happening to them.

* * *

When I started in the business, it was truly a man's world. Women need not apply. It was one of the most sexist businesses around. Women were secretaries, office help, and sex objects. It was *Mad Men* on steroids.

* * *

Back in those early days, before women became brokers, women in the business were usually young, beautiful, and impressionable. These were also the days of Woodstock, Haight-Ashbury, and free love. The late sixties and the early seventies were hedonistic times, and the brokerage business was no exception. It also seemed like there was a greater opportunity to party. When any excuse came along, we'd party.

Hiring standards were pretty loose and very sexist. If a woman could pass the pencil test, or the elbow test, they were pretty much assured of a job. If she were good-looking too, there was no way she wouldn't get hired.

For example, the three-martini lunch was pretty common, and many times, little work was accomplished in the afternoons at the office. At the same time, brokers usually had a lot of money in their pockets as most of them made good money and were paid pretty well. So you had the combination of beautiful young people, alcohol, money, sex, power, and lots of freedom. The results were fairly predictable.

On Friday afternoons, we used to party at the local watering hole with several brokers and a lot of secretaries. It was a wonderful time because everyone was trying to figure out who was going to go home with whom. Usually, it was kind of a foregone conclusion, but occasionally, especially when a new hire came aboard, the issue was debated at length. One particular afternoon I remember well. A broker named Dennis observed that two or three of us were particularly drawn to a certain young lady, and he came up with a brilliant idea: we'd pitch pennies to determine who would have the pleasure of taking this lucky lady to dinner and the inevitable next step. Everyone agreed that this was a superb idea, so three of us retired to a different room of the pub and proceeded to determine this secretary's program for the evening. I don't think she ever knew what machinations determined her date, and fate, for the evening.

It is also public record that one of the major brokerage firms had what they called the boom-boom room, a place in their building where they'd party in very explicit ways with any woman who'd care to participate. Eventually, someone blew the whistle, and the firm was nailed with a huge sexual harassment penalty, thereby ending that particular tradition.

Sex was good anytime, but it was especially good during bull markets. Making money in a big way is a powerful aphrodisiac. As Xaviera Hollender, a well-known Wall Street madam, once famously said, "When stocks go up, cocks go up."

Today, the business is so different that these things couldn't possibly happen. Oh, I'm certain that there are office romances, but the libertine life is gone forever. Now, the rule is "don't dip your pen in company ink," and "don't do your honey where you make your money." And finally, "Never have an affair with someone who has less to lose than you."

Sweat Equity and Other Lies

As a broker, you get to see a lot of money-making ideas. Most are nonsense, but some have merit. Telling the difference between the two is difficult, but the price of learning the difference is high. More money is flushed down the toilet by people who believe they have found the "next big thing." It cost me a ton of money before I made enough to make the education all worthwhile. If you're lucky, you will see a lot of these proposals, but you have to be careful. What follows are some of the things I have learned over the years. Pay attention. It could save you some money.

Back in 1980, before Microsoft Office, there was a company. Let's call it PAL, which invented the first spreadsheet. Remember, this was long before Excel and Lotus. I heard about this company and thought that this was a company worth investing in. So I made some inquiries, and lo and behold, I found a founder of the company who, although unwilling, said that he'd sacrifice and sell me a few thousand dollars of his personal stock. Well, that's lesson number 1: don't buy stock from an insider who is "forcing" himself to sell. What he's trying to do is unload something that he figures is soon going to be worthless. Well, to make a long and expensive story longer, a couple of weeks after we did the transaction, the guy who had the brains behind the software abandoned ship and joined Lotus for a lot of up-front dough, leaving PAL high, dry, and broke and without the intellect behind the great idea. Those of us who bought stock had no recourse but to lick our wounds and dream of what could have been.

Sometime in the '90s, another scheme came along: a better, energy-efficient "mousetrap." This one was a little more expensive, but I trusted the people who were involved. The main man, let's call him Jacque, was bright, persuasive, articulate, and related to a man whom I had known for a long time. Well, it took several years before the company burned through, if you can believe it, some 15 million dollars before, as Jacque liked to put it, "We'll hit the wall going ninety miles an hour." It's hard to say why we burned through so much money because it was difficult, if not impossible, to see where the money was spent. Lesson number 2: don't invest just because you think you know the people involved. This guy not only screwed several of us, but his relatives got screwed royally too. Jacque went to another state and disappeared probably with a big hunk of the $15 million.

The biggest lie, however, is "sweat equity." I've seen so many ideas come before me looking for financing that I've lost count. I've seen a lot of people put money into things that never paid off. I've seen a lot of sophisticated brokers and investors believe "the story" and wind up losing their butt. Their investments turned into what I call "whale turds," sinking slowly to the bottom of the ocean. Actually, I don't know if whale turds sink or float, but I really like the imagery. It took me a long time to learn that "sweat equity" is a code word for not having any real financial interest in the project. I've learned another important lesson: when you hear "sweat equity," run, don't walk, away from the investment. If you ask, "How much skin do you have in the game?" and you don't like the answer, or if you hear "sweat equity," get the hell away from that project. In case you don't know what "skin in the game means," it means cold, hard, real money, cash. If you hear, "I want you to invest because I have $50,000 of sweat equity in this project," the dude is just looking for you to pay his salary for a while before he goes away.

And by the way, making money in start-ups is incredibly difficult. A wise man, a founder of several start-ups, once told me that when something interesting came along, put some money into it, but be prepared to lose 3 out of 4 deals. He said that the fourth deal would make the other losses all worthwhile. He was right.

What he didn't say, and what I've learned and will to pass it along in the hope that it'll save you all some money, is that it's real important to see who the other players in the venture are. If you've looked at the deal and see some other sophisticated folk putting skin in the game, and you still have the chance to buy some stock, you at least have a fighting chance to make some money. The best kind of folk to have preceding you are those who've done it before. The problem is, however, that these guys form a rather tight club, and it's very hard to have anybody let you in. A good rule of thumb is if it's easy to get in, it probably is going to cost you a lot of lost money in the long run. This is a real good reason to build yourself a network of friends who know what they're doing.

The next problem and one that requires a lot of discipline on your part is time. Time is a relative term, but if you put some skin in the game, you should be prepared to wait five to seven years before things get interesting. You'll either be "in the boat" or "out of the boat" by that time, and there are no guarantees either way.

I had a woman come to me not so long ago, and I'm not making this up, who told me that she had a great way to make money over the Internet. She was going to create a website called DigitalDumps and appeal to the prurient interests of people who were fascinated by excrement. She assumed that there were lot of people who were fascinated by this who would pay good money to purchase digital photos of turds. She said, "We could have excrement photos from females, males, animals of all kinds, politicians we didn't like, politicians we liked, movie stars, fish, and from people around the world. Who knows how much money we could make if we were able to get photos of the dumps of famous people?" Why, we could create a whole new industry. The paparazzi would have a whole new field to follow. Now celebrities could be followed everywhere in the hopes that they would leave a calling card behind, so to speak. I asked about how she could know if a celebrity pile was counterfeit or not, and how she might be able to get a certificate of authenticity, and finally, I allowed as how this was an interesting and provocative idea, but when she told me that all she had in it was sweat equity, and so to speak, I passed on the idea. It was another idea that went in the toilet.

I think that the lesson to be learned here is that it's very difficult to make money in start-ups, but in order to have a chance, you have to follow the money and the people who are smarter than you are and are willing to put "skin in the game."

Many Are Called . . .

Millions of people have money in the securities' markets. Most people have representation through their 401(k)s or other retirement plans. Yet it's still astounding how little people actually know about how markets work. It's also amazing to me how people underestimate how much money they'll actually need to finance a reasonable retirement.

It's even stranger to me how some stupid clients never listen to a broker (stupid or otherwise), who can give them good advice. Then, they turn around and don't do anything. "It's too slow" seems to be a recurring refrain. The popular news media seems to be part and parcel of a vast conspiracy to keep people poor. It's not only the advertisements that encourage people to *trade* over the Internet on the cheap. "Hey, your first twenty-five Internet trades are free, and we'll even put $100 into your account to make it easy. We even have live people you can talk to who can give you advice in real time." What is this crap? It's hard for even the best brains on Wall Street to make money consistently when they trade.

* * *

Risk

It's hard to figure out what kind of diversification is desirable for a person's given amount of risk tolerance. You first have to figure out how much risk you're willing to take for a given amount of return. There are ways to figure this, but you'll need a good advisor to help you.

Back in the late 1990s and the early 2000s, before the Internet bubble burst, most people had no clue as to what risk tolerance they really had. "Oh, I don't mind risk," said the stupid clients to their stupid brokers. "I'm diversified," said the stupid client who thought owning Intel, Cisco, Applied Materials, HP, IBM, Cypress Semi, Juniper, Arriba, plus a few other Internet stocks made for a diversified portfolio. Vertically integrated diversification in the same asset class never did much for me. When the bubble burst, everything went down. These folk got their heads handed to them.

Then, there are my favorite people who believe that markets always go in a straight line. In a good market, zillions of people sit behind their Excel program and do straight-line appreciation at 12, 15, or even 20% a year. At these compounding rates, money grows in a big hurry. Soon, you'll have all the money in the world. These are the people who are like lambs to the slaughter. They put a few thousand dollars into their portfolios and think that they are on the road to easy street. The idea absolutely makes me crazy, but this is the way many people, new to the markets, do their math. I call it the new math only because with computers, it makes the compounding easier. It only leads to overconfidence, greed, and disaster.

When the bubble burst and the hysteria subsided in 2000, people lost an awful lot of money. Most of these people will never return to direct investing in the market. They'll be content with their 401(k)s or other IRA-type accounts, put their minimum contributions in, and leave the dollars in a money market fund where their investment is safe, but totally unproductive. It's only during the next big bull market that these timid souls will take their money and put it into equities or other growth situations. Once again, they'll "buy high and sell low." I call it the "I gotta hunch, let's go to lunch and then buy a bunch" school of investing.

Oh, we don't want to pay a good broker some percentage to share her wisdom garnered after fighting the wars for years, but we'll do it on our own and lose our asses, once again.

The "moving finger writes, and having writ, moves on." So it is with the market. "Many are called . . ., and most of them lose their butts."

... And Few Are Chosen

So why is it so difficult to make money in the market? Why is it so difficult to accumulate wealth? Why, why, why? We've talked about it earlier, but I believe all the clichés and redundant observations are true. "We don't plan to fail, we just fail to plan." How many of you are sitting there, right now, saying, "You just don't understand. It's impossible to save any money"? A lot of people float through life, blissfully unaware of the inexorable march of time. "Time is money; money is time," says a good friend of mine who's a smart client. Why does he say that? Well . . .

There is a concept called the "time value of money."

* * *

My dad was a man of action and very few words. He never finished high school because he had to go to work for a living, but he had a vast knowledge of life and a witty saying for almost any situation. One of my favorites was when he said that, "The first million dollars is the hardest to make." I didn't understand that until I made my first million, but it's absolutely true. He worked for wages all his life and never got to a net worth of a million dollars, but then, that was back in the days when a million dollars was worth something. But he was absolutely right. Once you have a million dollars on the net worth side of your ledger, it becomes easier to make the second million and the third and so on . . . All you need is *time*!

Pay attention now, so you can quit being a stupid client or stupid broker and start understanding how you can get smart. If you think you're a stupid client, don't worry because very few brokers understand what we're going to talk about right now, and this contains the seminal kernel of truth that really makes people rich.

"Oh," you might say, "I don't really want to be rich." Well, if that's your attitude, quit wasting my time! And yours! Stay the hell away from the securities' markets because you're just going to lose your butt anyway. Furthermore, you will not be willing to do what it takes to get rich. But please buy my book, and put it on your coffee table so people will think you're smart.

There are several kinds of interest in life. In the old days, we used to take a lot of interest in the secretaries in the office, and they in us, but we're not talking about this kind of interest. We're going to talk about money interest.

The first kind of interest is simple interest. The concept is simple, and I'll try to keep it that way. Let's say, you have $1,000. Someone is going to pay you 10% simple interest a year. After the first year, you will have $1,100. After the second year, you will have earned another $100, so your total will be $1,200. This goes on for 10 years, at which time you will have a total of $2,000. This is not only very boring, but it's not the kind of interest you want to have.

Baron Von Rothschild, one of the smartest and richest men of all time and the creator of one of the world's great all-time fortunes, said that the greatest invention of all time was the concept of compound interest. This is what we're going to talk about, and as far as I'm concerned, this is the secret. Everything else we'll talk about depends on this concept, so pay attention.

Let's go back to our original $1,000, only this time, we'll get 10% interest compounded annually. After the first year, we'll still have the same $1,100, but watch what happens in year 2. Whereas in the first example, we had $1,200, with compound interest, we'd have $1,210 [(1,100 × 10%) + 1,100 or (110 + 1,100 = 1,210)]. This may not seem very exciting, but instead of waiting 10 years to get to a total of $2,000, you will get to $2,000 after only 7.2 years. At the end of 10 years, you will have a total of $2,593. So you'd be $593 ahead of where you'd been with just simple interest. Magic!

You still might be tempted to say, "Gee, it was only an additional $593 after ten years." Well, you're right, but suppose you'd started with $1,000,000. You would have an additional $593,000, and that, as they say, "Ain't hay."

Let's learn another trick of the trade. This one is simply called the rule of 72. "What," you might say, "is the rule of 72?" It is a simple and quick aid that allows you to roughly figure how long it will take your money to double at any certain interest rate; i.e., if you have a 10% compound interest rate, your money will double in 7.2 years. If you get 8% compounded, your money will double in 9 years. With 6%, it'll double in 12 years. This is precisely why it is so important to maximize your returns. Let's look at a couple of further examples: At 4%, 18 years. At 5%, 14+ years. At 6%, 12 years. At 9%, 8 years. This may seem trivial to the casual student, but let's take a lifetime of investing, say 45 years. On a $10,000 investment, left alone without further additions of capital, after 45 years, will grow to $89,000+ at 5%. The same $10,000 at 6% will grow to $137,000. At 7% to $210,000. At 10% to $728,000 and at 12%, a whopping $1,639,000. The smart client will immediately understand why a difference of +1% or +5% can make a huge difference in the outcome over time.

So what does this mean to the average investor who starts out her adult life without a great deal of money? Unfortunately, in my experience, it doesn't mean much. I don't know the percentage of people who don't have a clue about compound interest and the power it holds for individuals who want to get wealthy, but I bet it is huge.

Actually, the numbers work in favor of the investor as long as the investing starts early in a career. Remember, there are no guarantees, and the numbers are hypothetical, but if history is our guide, and it's the only guide we have, the stock market has returned an average of about 10% for 100 years. So we'll make some assumptions. Obviously, it is not a straight-line appreciation, although some people believe that it should be.

KING MIDAS

If a person starts saving $4,000 a year in a tax-deferred account, and we'll use tax-deferred accounts, like an IRA, because it's a lot easier to make calculations than if we took taxes into consideration.

Let's say that person A puts $4,000 a year into this account starting at age 26 and continues at $4,000 a year until age 65. This person will have accumulated almost $1,800,000. This results from contributions totaling $160,000 and compounding at 10% a year.

Now, let's say that person B puts the same $4,000 a year into this account each year beginning at age 19 and continues until age 26 and then never contributes another dime. At age 65, this person will have accumulated almost $1,900,000 for a total contribution of just $28,000.

Now, let's take a very smart teenager who starts putting money away at age 14 and continues through age 18. This is a total contribution of $20,000 and never puts in another dime. This sum will grow to almost $2,300,000 at age 65.

Investor D has very smart parents, and they put away a total of $14,000 by the time baby reaches age 13. Then, no more money is contributed, and the money is allowed to grow until baby reaches age 65. This total will reach about $2,500,000.

Investor E follows the pattern of the child in "D" and continues to invest $4,000 a year until age 65. This total grows to an astounding $8,600,000.

Now, you are probably shaking your head and wondering how anybody could plan so far ahead and that you are incapable of doing it. Well, I will go on the record and say that you are totally wrong. Maybe you are older and are getting a late start. That's possible, but you probably are making more money and can afford to put more money away.

The next excuse that I'm totally tired of hearing from stupid clients is that they are incapable of saving any money. "Oh," says the stupid client, "I can't save a dime because I need it all." This is where you need a reality check by examining your budget and your spending habits. Let me give you an example: Suppose you stop by your local coffee shop, and your barista gets you a coffee and doughnut every day as you head for work. Let's say it costs you about $3 a day to do this. Do you know that if you just skipped one day a week and took this $3 and put it into the stock market, that after 40 years, you would have about $65,000? Anybody can save $3 a week.

What other things could you do to save some money without much effort? Try always buying the cheapest gasoline. Your car will probably run just as well, and you'll save money. Try buying well drinks instead of Sam Daniels or Chivas until you can afford the more expensive brands. Better yet, don't drink and bank the money. Don't buy expensive cars. One of the reasons I quit smoking forty years ago was because I did a future value using calculating the time value of money. At that time, a pack of cigs cost about 35 cents. I had about a dollar-a-day habit, and I figured that after 40 years, I would burn up about $75,000. Today, with the cost of a pack of cigarettes north of $6, you'd burn up over a million bucks.

Having a Blueprint

Otherwise Known as a Game Plan

Let's see! Vince Lombardi shows up for an important Green Bay Packer playoff game at Lambeau Field and is asked what his game plan is. John Madden overhears him say that the team, on this particular Sunday, was going to play it by ear. "I don't know," he says. "We'll just have to see what develops. I think we'll make it up as we go along." John Madden goes back to the broadcasting booth and is apoplectic. In his famous way, he throws up his hands and shouts that he can't believe it, and "Lombardi must have lost his mind."

General Dwight D. Eisenhower, in preparing for D-day in 1944, was in charge of the greatest sea invasion in history. His staff couldn't believe it when he designed the plans for the assault on the back of an envelope. (Does this sound like the business plans for some of the dot-coms during the Internet bubble?) He was responsible for thousands of ships, hundreds of thousands of men and women, zillions of tons of supplies, and a ream of opportunities for the attack on Hitler's Festung Europa.

Do the two examples above sound stupid? You bet they do, and thank goodness, they never happened. Lombardi never ever went into a game unprepared, and General Eisenhower spent years huddling with his generals and staff preparing detailed plans for the invasion of Europe.

What's the similarity between the two? They were very successful, and they had carefully thought out game plans.

I don't care whether it's a plan for a small business, a road trip across the country, a hiking trip through the mountains, building a house, charting a career path, or figuring out how you are going to create enough wealth to protect you in your retirement, whether early or not.

You need a financial blueprint! You have to figure out what you have to do to get to your goals!

* * *

Over the decades, whenever I would meet with a client, or a potential client, one of the first questions I'd ask was what their financial goals were. The usual answer, which was no help at all, was "to make money."

"No, no," I'd say.

"Where do you want to be in five years? Ten years? Thirty years?"

"Rich" or "a lot" was the usual reply.

"How much money is that?" I'd ask.

Unfortunately, their answer was usually pretty nebulous and worthless.

"What's your net worth?" was another question. Most people have no clue what that means. "What's that?" they would say. I'll bet that you, gentle reader, if you have waded through the book this far, might have a clue about net worth. However, if you need a definition, it's fairly simple: You add up everything you own, subtract the things you owe, and find your net worth. This is important because it gives you a starting point.

Unfortunately, most people have little or a negative net worth. I had a stupid client once, a doctor, who had been in practice for several years. He was a nice guy, bright and personable. I went through the drill with him and couldn't believe when we finished, that he had (including his house which was fully mortgaged) a net worth of about $25,000. I then began to talk about where he wanted to go, and he said, "Aren't you going to ask me about my credit cards?"

At that point, I felt like a stupid broker because it hadn't occurred to me to ask this particular question. "How much are you running on your cards?" I asked.

"Oh, about $55,000," he replied.

That gave him a negative net worth of $30,000. At that point, I told him that I really couldn't help him until he got out of debt, provided for an emergency fund of $30,000, and got a pile of money that he could invest. I never got him as a client. I don't know what happened to him, but I've made a habit of asking about credit card debt ever since.

Rule number 1: Pay off your credit cards monthly. Pay as you go!

Over the years, I have occasionally seen a client carry a significant balance on a credit card and roll it over every month while paying the minimum. This is very expensive and makes money for no one except the credit card company. Once in a while, a stupid client will be paying the credit card issuer somewhere north of 18% while having a savings account paying them a couple of percent. This makes no sense whatsoever, so if you find yourself in this situation, pay off your credit cards, and don't carry any sort of balance. Use your savings account to pay off your credit card debt if you have to.

Rule number 2: Cut up most of your credit cards, and don't run up balances that you can't pay off on a monthly basis.

Getting back to the blueprint for a moment, what you have to do is decide where you want to be one year from now, two years from now, five years from now, and when you retire. Basically, the question to ask is this: "How much money am I going to need, and how am I going to get it?" If you want to retire with $2,000,000, you need to crunch the numbers to see how much you have to put away in order to get there.

But then you have to take into account all the things that can go wrong between here and there: for example, (1) children; (2) divorces; (3) getting screwed; (4) bad investments; (5) uninsured losses from fire, earthquake, flood, or other natural disasters; 6) buying a house; 7) taking care of a house; and 8) anything else that can go wrong. I figure that you must make allowance for at least three major setbacks during your lifetime. As the old saying goes, "Stuff happens!" and you have to prepare for it.

Let's take them one at a time. First, children! A lot of people decide to have children without even considering the cost of raising the cute little devils. At the time of this writing, 2015, the cost of raising a kiddo and getting her through college is estimated at about $250,000. So you must figure out how you're going to manage that and how that fits into the rest of your plan. Then, you must ask yourself at what point you're going to consider the kids launched. I've known many clients who never manage to launch them. The kids are still hanging around, swilling from their parents' trough, the bank of Mom and Dad, throughout middle age.

Second, divorces. About 50% of all marriages end in divorce. Divorces are expensive. The cute, loving wife or studly husband, instead of participating in a life of wedded bliss, can turn into your worst enemy. As the old saying goes, "Marriage is like a tornado. At first there is a lot of sucking and blowing, and then you lose your house." If you get divorced in most states, you have to split up almost all your assets from your blessed partnership. This, coupled with the trauma of splitting up your family, can be a huge disaster for most people because a lot of the expenses just keep rolling on. You still have to take care of the children, pay, or receive child support, pay or receive alimony, pay the attorneys, etc. My advice, don't do it. Some people ignore this and do it two or three times. As my mother-in-law likes to say, "Divorce never! Murder, maybe!" Don't do that either. Prison makes it even worse even though most of your expenses are paid for.

The third trap is getting screwed. This can take many forms from bad investments to loaning money to your brother-in-law. We've already talked about some forms of bad investments. It's important to avoid those traps, but I'd like to mention a couple more: penny stocks and deals that sound too good to be true are generally too good to be true. I can't tell you how many stupid clients buy shares in stocks selling under $2. I don't do it for them anymore because it is just throwing money away. Stocks, after getting so low, almost never come back. People say that all they can lose is $1.25 a share, but it bears repeating that it is still 100% of their dough, and they have to live with that stuff on their statements forever as it's almost impossible to get the certificates for a stock selling that cheap, so it shows up every month on your monthly statement, forever reminding you of your stupidity, again . . . and . . . again . . . and again . . .

From time to time, I get a call from a stupid client who wants me to help them chase down a firm that sold them some gold, cattle, coins, etc. The client sent his/her money to them and never got anything in return. I don't know why people would sometimes rather buy stuff from some unknown person who calls out of the blue than from an established broker, but they do. I usually just refer them to the National Association of Security Dealers complaint division, but their money is gone nevertheless.

I forget who said it first, but it's true, "A fool and his money are soon parted."

You have to be careful. There are people out there who will gladly take your dough, and they won't even say thank you. There are people who don't know squat about investing and will sell you a bill of goods. Look, it's easy enough to make stupid investments with the best of intentions. Don't be foolish.

The fourth trap is making bad investments. As Will Rogers famously once said, "Only buy investments that go up. If they don't go up, don't buy them." I think we've covered this topic, but don't be stupid and buy junk. Buy good stuff, preferably that pays a good dividend, and hang on. You'll make enough mistakes by accident. Don't make them on purpose.

The fifth trap is insurance, or more properly said, the lack thereof. One of my favorite insurance consultants has a sage comment regarding insurance. He is fond of saying that "the day you *really* need insurance is the day you can't have it." Think about that for a minute. Let's say you're like a lot of stupid clients, and for several years, you've been thinking about getting some life insurance to protect your family just in case you happen to get on the wrong plane or something. But like most everyone, you've put it off. Then, one day, you go to the doctor, and she tells you, you have something that's going to kill you in six months, and you should go home and get your estate in order. Don't laugh! It happens all the time. So you say to yourself, "Self, you'd better get some life insurance to protect your family." Your insurance agent tells you that, "You can't have it because you're uninsurable. Neener, neener, neener." Actually, he's thinking that you are totally a dumb shit because you never listened to him when you could have gotten it with no problem.

The same thing holds true for car insurance, home insurance, health insurance, etc. If you lose your house in a flood or earthquake, and you don't have any flood or earthquake insurance, you ain't gonna get it after the fact. In fact, in 1989, a friend had been thinking about getting earthquake insurance on his house and finally got around to calling his insurance guy. This was on a Tuesday morning, and they made an appointment to get together on Friday. Well, the biggest earthquake in eighty-five years hit the Bay Area that Tuesday afternoon at 5:07 and ultimately did about $75,000 worth of damage to his house. He was a day late and a dollar short, but such is the luck of the draw and the cost of procrastination.

The sixth and seventh traps are similar in that they regard buying a home. I can't tell you how many people tell me that their house is the best investment that they ever made. Well, I'm here to tell you that a house is a terrible, but necessary investment. It is what's commonly known as a "use asset." You need it, but it costs you a ton of money. Certainly, it's better than renting because you are building equity, and it works kind of like an enforced savings plan, assuming of course that you pay down the mortgage. It costs you insurance, taxes, upkeep, paint, plumbing, gardening, landscaping, furniture, rugs, insulation, and all the other tons of stuff you need to keep your house going. Then, of course, something breaks, or the roof leaks, and you have to dig deep into your emergency fund, which of course you may or may not have because your stupid broker neglected to recommend that you save money for just such emergencies.

An especially insidious trap is the eighth one. This is the curse of monthly payments. This is the one that will sneak up on you and, without warning, will overwhelm your careful plans for saving. You know the kind of payments I'm talking about. For example, your cell phone: $70/month; your satellite TV: $50/month; your house insurance: $70/month; your car payments and insurance: $400/month; your iTunes purchases: $40/month; your home telephone: $45/month; your electricity, water, gas, etc.: $200 month, if you're lucky; your fitness gym: $30/month; your magazine subscriptions, including newspapers: about $75/month; your Internet connection: about $70/month. And I'm sure you have a number of others, if you stop to look. It's so easy to say that "It's only $20 a month, I can afford that." Well, if we take a moment and add up the above numbers, we have a total of $1,050 a month. In other words, it's really easy to nickel and dime yourself to death without even trying. It's critically important to monitor and limit your "monthlies." It ain't for nothing that these advertisements on television tout products for $19.99 as that number seems to be just below the threshold of pain. Most people don't even notice how many $20–$25 a month payments they have. What's worse is that you sometimes forget how many of these payments are done automatically, and you actually forget that you have them. Cancel a credit card once in a while, and you'll see how many places call you up for a missed payment. You'll be surprised!

The ninth trap is anything else that can go wrong. Just spend some time thinking about it. All kinds of stuff can happen. If you spend your life worrying about everything, you'll go nuts. So don't worry because you probably can't do anything about it anyway. But be prepared. As the old saying goes, "Shit happens."

So where does that leave us? We've set some goals. We've developed a plan for getting there. We know it's going to take some time, but we're going to be patient and intentional about our task. We have made plans to contact a smart broker who will take some time and educate us about what we have to do. We'll be sure to tell her that we won't waste her time, and that we'll eventually have a significant amount of money to invest. We'll reevaluate our game plan every year or so to see if we have to make any course corrections. And we'll be prepared to save more money if we have to.

Getting Into the Habit

What does intentionality mean?

It means that the earlier you decide that you want to be wealthy, (and you can define wealthy any way you want), and dedicate yourself to that goal, you will develop the lifestyle that will get you there. Parenthetically, wealthy might just mean that you don't want to be like two-thirds of retirees who quit working with little more income than just Social Security.

This way of lifestyle has what I like to call the "stickiness" factor. When you think about your personal cash flow, you begin to realize that money comes in, from whatever source, although it's usually from wages or salaries, flows through your life and is paid out to support your way of life. In a way, it's like putting on weight or dieting. You feed your face, digest your food, and then excrete the remainder. If you scarf more than you evacuate, then you'll put on weight. If you evacuate more than you eat, you'll lose weight. See, the food sticks to your body.

It's the same with money. If you make more than you spend, the surplus sticks to your investments and your accounts. If you spend more than you make, you'll be in debt, and your accounts will look funny because there'll be a lot of minus signs or red numbers mucking up the pages. If you spend all you make, you'll never see your accounts grow.

So if you're serious, you'll try to get some money to stick to your portfolio. You want those accounts to grow. If you don't want to do this, a smart broker will not want to waste her time on you. If you don't get into the habit early, you certainly won't get into it later.

Remember, there are three ways to get rich:

1. Inherit it or marry it. This is the lucky-sperm concept.

2. Get lucky. Go to work for a start-up in its early days or win the lottery

3. Do it the old-fashioned way. Earn it and save it.

The habits, as we've discussed before, are important enough to talk about again. You don't need the most expensive of anything. Buy the cheaper grade of gas. Buy the cheaper latte. You don't need the most expensive car. Until you have a good nest egg put away, buy a preowned car. You'll be amazed at the money you'll save. If you happen to get a windfall from a sale of an asset, don't spend it all but put it into your investments. If you are too weak to do that, put at least half of it into your portfolio. If you get a raise at work, take half of it and invest it regularly. Use the other half to improve your lifestyle. Better yet, if you have the strength, put it all away. Remember, the early money is the best money because it has longer to grow because of compound interest.

A good rule of thumb is simply that if you're not saving at least 15% of whatever you're making, you're not saving enough.

Gold

As I write this, gold is off about $500 an ounce from its past highs. Usually, the price of gold is a sign that there is great uncertainty in the world, and/or inflation is about ready to rear its ugly head. Whenever gold begins to make a significant move, it's time to pay attention. Having said that, I want to refresh your memories about the history of gold during the last thirty or thirty-five years. For a long time, the US government stood ready to buy all the gold proffered to it at $32 an ounce. Dick Nixon closed the gold window about 1973 and let the price of gold float freely. Probably a decent idea, but it removed the discipline that a fixed price of gold imposed on the government. In other words, the government was free to print as much money, called fiat money, as it wanted, and it caused the great inflation of the late 1970s and early 1980s. The price of gold moved from $32 an ounce to about $800 an ounce, and every gold bug in the world was out telling people how the world was coming to an end and that everyone should be buying gold. Lots of these guys made a lot of money on the lecture circuit and by selling books.

A lot of stupid clients went out and bought as much gold as they could at prices above $600 an ounce. Then, they watched it all come apart, and gold sank to about $250 an ounce and sat there for fifteen years. Now it's moving again, and just watch the gold bugs start crowing again.

Owning gold and other precious metals has its own cachet. It's fun to say that you own a bunch of gold. You can buy bullion, coins, bars, and nuggets. I always wonder who's doing the selling to the suckers who are buying. If it were such a great investment, they wouldn't be selling it. Precious metals have their own problems. You have to pay storage and insurance. If you take delivery of bullion, you have to have it assayed if you want to sell it back. You can't eat it, and it doesn't pay dividends. It just kind of sits there consuming money, and all you can do is hope it goes up.

Let's say it does go from its present $1,100 an ounce to $2,000 an ounce, and you are fortunate enough to sell it. Where do you go from there? All of a sudden, after paying taxes on the gain, you have dollar bills again and basically nowhere to put them. So, usually, gold becomes sort of a self-fulfilling prophecy, and you own it forever. My advice? If you're worried, buy some pretty gold coins and make jewelry out of them. At least you can wear them.

As part of a diversified portfolio, it probably doesn't hurt to own them, but a good commodities' fund is probably the best way to play fear of inflation.

Investing Strategies

When I first started in the business, investing was pretty simple: you could invest in common and preferred stocks, taxable and nontaxable bonds, and mutual funds. Back in those days, you could establish a relationship with an experienced broker and stick with him for a long time. This broker would understand you and try to establish what kind of risks you wanted to take. The more important thing, however, was his helping determine how much risk was really suitable for you.

    I think one of the most important things you can do when you're starting out is to start out conservatively. Don't "go to lunch, get a hunch, and buy a bunch." What we're going to do from here on out is to talk about the steps you should take to begin to build your fortune, assuming that you want one. If you don't want one, put the book down, and go play because what we're going to do now is learn important stuff.

    It would be nice if you could walk into a brokerage firm and hook up with a good man or woman who has some experience on Wall Street. If you're lucky enough to have some $50,000 to $100,000 in investable cash or securities lying around, don't just walk into a firm and ask to see a broker. As I've said, you'll usually wind up with the greenest person on "duty" that day. This isn't always bad, as a younger broker is often hungry and can afford to spend time with you; however, I think a person who is not a professional in the field needs some good advice and some direction from a more seasoned broker.

The best advice is to go up to the front desk and ask to see the manager. The manager, or assistant manager, will chat with you for a while, and you should ask her to match you up with a broker who has a similar personality and specializes in helping people get started accumulating assets. Don't be concerned if you have to interview two or three brokers before you find one you like.

This is precisely why I think the advertisements on the TV are so misleading and downright counterproductive when it comes to helping people accumulate wealth. I've always maintained that the worst possible thing that can happen to a new client is to pick a stock that turns out to be a winner. What this does is create a false sense of security and leads people to believe that picking stocks and making money is easy. *It ain't*. Then, you get these commercials from some dippy brokerage firm that lead you to believe that all you need is some sophisticated, off-the-shelf software, and twenty-five free Internet trades, and you are on your way. *Wrong!*

If you are lucky enough to find a broker who will spend some time with you, thank your lucky stars. More than likely, you'll remember back in the earlier chapters when we discussed how a broker can't really afford to spend time with non-income-producing people. If you have some assets and you are committed to saving and investing, you may convince the broker to invest some time in you.

If you are like most people, however, you won't have a lot of money to start with. You might, in fact, have some debt left over from college, some maxed-out credit cards (pay them off and burn them!), and some car payments, etc. In other words, you have dug yourself a hole and don't really know how to get out of it. The first rule when you have dug a hole for yourself is to *quit digging*. This is where your self-respect and self-determination come in. Most people never stop digging, and their hole just gets deeper and deeper and deeper . . .

So let's assume that you've become serious about investing and accumulating wealth. What do you do now? If you've got a good broker or financial planner, great! If you don't, I suggest you get some of the great books that are out there, starting with this one.

The first thing to do is to figure out how much money you can save each month. If you can't save enough so it begins to hurt, you're not saving enough. Over the years, I've heard it all. People say they need all their money to live on. They just can't possibly save anything. They really need that new car or that Gucci handbag. They need the thousand-dollar golf clubs or skis. They just have to take that trip to the Caribbean and play for a week at Club Med. They just have to have their double mocha each day to preserve their mental health. You should look through your lifestyle and decide on your priorities. Do you want instant gratification, or do you want to be intentional about getting rich? When you're rich, you can look back at when you were poor and decide that, and I forget who said it first, "I've been poor, and I've been rich. Rich is better."

So you've decided to grow up and get serious. What do you do? I think the first thing you should do is to get out of debt. Pay off your credit cards, your car and college loans. Then, cut up your credit cards, and throw them away. Quit paying other people exorbitant rates of interest and start putting some of that money into your own pockets. Remember the stickiness factor. It isn't going to stick to you or your brokerage account if you're paying it out to other folk. At the same time, and this is where it begins to hurt, you should start building an emergency fund.

Another very important thing that you should do when you buy stocks is to get into the habit of reinvesting your dividends. Most brokerage firms will now do that for you at no cost. It is a painless way to save more money, and it'll help your portfolio grow faster.

Another good method is dollar-cost averaging. This means that you should invest on a specific time schedule no matter what the market is doing. Some people just put money into the market whenever they have some cash on hand. Over time, this lowers your cost basis and improves your rate of return.

The Emergency Fund

An emergency fund is just what the name implies. It's a fund to be used for emergencies. "Like what?" you may ask. Like if your car breaks down, you lose your job, you break your leg, or heaven forbid, you forgot to purchase insurance, and something unforeseen happens. Even young people get sick, friends, so even though you think you might not need it, health insurance has to be an integral part of any serious plan. Obamacare makes health insurance mandatory.

You ask, "How much should I have in my emergency fund?" Here the answer is never concrete. Most planners I know think that three to six months of earnings should be kept in a safe place. This means that it should be in a money market fund or very short-term certificates of deposit. It means that it should be somewhere where you can get to it quickly and without taking any market risks.

Then, and only then, after you're out of debt and have an established emergency fund are you ready to begin investing. Before you do that, however, without invading your fund, reward yourself for a job well done. Go out and have a nice dinner with friends and begin to look ahead for the accumulation phase of your road to riches.

The 401(k)

When you go to work, as most of us do, one of the first benefits you are usually offered is a retirement plan called the 401(k). The hard thing is that you are offered this at the very time when you are starting out with about zero assets. That makes it difficult to make the decision to take 2, 4, 6, or 10% of your income and put it into the plan. Fortunately, you have the good sense to take this monumental step, as it will put you on the correct path to accumulate a ton of money by the time you are old and gray.

This is one of the best things you can take advantage of while you're building your nest egg for your eventual retirement. Unfortunately, even with its many benefits, an astounding number of individuals fail to sign up. An even more astounding number of people fail to fund it to the max. Don't be dumb! Join your 401(k).

There are many reasons that you should join your company's plan, and they're all good. In the first place, it usually requires that you make regular payments with pretax dollars into the plan, and this alone helps you to save money automatically on a continuing basis. This gives you all the benefits of dollar-cost averaging, which is just a way of buying securities whether the market is up or down. Remember that we talked about early money being the best money, and it's important to put as large a percent of your income into the plan as you can.

Another major advantage is the fact that contributions to a 401(k) reduce the amount of your taxable income, and you don't have to pay income tax on that money, even though you've earned it. Furthermore, any investments made with your contributions grow on a tax-deferred basis. In other words, you don't have to pay any current income tax on the growth of your funds. You will have to pay taxes on your withdrawals made at age 59½. Withdrawals made before 59½ are subject, in most cases, to a 10% penalty as well as income tax. You must begin withdrawals at age 70½.

The biggest advantage, however, and this is not true with every company, is the simple fact that your employer may match, sometimes dollar for dollar up to a certain point, every dollar you put in. This money is not yours immediately, but it becomes yours after a certain period, which can vary from company to company. When you are "vested," the money is yours if you leave the company for greener pastures somewhere else.

Then, we come to another advantage. If you leave the company, you can take your money, plus your vested share, with you. You can put your money into the new company's plan, or you can roll it over into your own individual retirement account. I think it's very important to make sure you take this money with you because then you are able to control it. Sometimes, and I've seen this one, stupid clients leave their money behind in the old company's plans and then have a hard time getting to it when they need it. I used to have one stupid client who had never moved her 401(k)s even though she had been with six different companies. I recommended that she get all of them consolidated into one IRA, and she never did. Someday, when she retires, she's going to have one heck of a time getting all the money that she's entitled to. She wasn't even sure if the companies were still in business or had merged with new companies. When she starts making the calls, she's going to find out that she will be very low on the priority lists of the companies that she'd left. Her request will go to the bottom of the pile, and she'll become a very, very frustrated person. As you might imagine, I finally fired her. Why should I continue to deal with a person who repeatedly fails to take very sensible suggestions?

Anyway, a 401(k) is something that you should definitely take advantage of. The only other point I want to make is that you must make sure that your money is properly allocated among one or more good equity funds. Most every employer will offer you several to choose from, and you should consult a good broker who will recommend a proper assortment and allocation for you. Remember, you are in this for the long term, and time is your friend. It's amazing how money will grow especially when your employer is helping your nest egg by putting company money into your account. Even so, many stupid clients wind up putting their money into a simple money market fund where they get the minimum growth possible, most of the time not even keeping up with inflation.

As of this writing, there is something called a Roth 401(k). This is similar, but different. Instead of making a tax-deductible contribution to your 401(k), the money goes in without a deduction. This allows the money to compound on a tax-free basis because when you take the money out, unlike a regular 401(k), you pay no taxes on the withdrawals.

Participate in your 401(k)! When your working life is over, you will be very pleased the day they give you your gold watch.

Plan of Attack

Like fighting a modern war using ships, planes, tanks, infantry, helicopters, and missiles, you are fighting a battle to amass enough money to provide you and your loved ones with a comfortable living sometime in the future. This does not mean that you can't live comfortably while you are putting your fortune together, but it means that as you get older, and your pile of dough grows, you will be able to buy bigger and better things, take bigger and better trips, and have bigger and better toys. Remember, we're talking about getting money and the things that money can buy.

While you're building, and protecting, your pile, you should use all the tools at your disposal. If you do, you'll be successful.

Regular IRAs and Roth IRAs

If you are really serious about building a nest egg, you should, in addition to fully funding your 401(k), you should put as much money as you can early on into your IRAs.

They kind of work like your 401(k), but the contribution limits are different. The regular IRA is tax deductible when you put money into it and taxable when you withdraw it. The Roth IRA is nontax deductible when you put money into it and non-taxable when you withdraw it. I personally think that the Roth IRA is a license given to you by the government that practically lets you steal.

XXIV

Getting Your First House

The great American Dream is having your own house, and this should be an important goal for anyone who is trying to develop a balanced portfolio. Homeownership is a very satisfying and gratifying thing to strive for. It's a place where you'll probably live with your significant other, raise your children, build equity, and be on the hook to the county for taxes and to the bank for thirty years of mortgage payments.

Furthermore, you will have to spend a ton of money for upkeep, maintenance, furniture, washers and dryers, televisions, new stuff that somebody's going to want. Things break and must be replaced. Lawns need mowing, mold grows in walls, insurance needs to be purchased to protect the largest investment that most people will ever make in their lifetime, and in short, as wonderful as it is, it is a money sinkhole that will suck money out of your wallet for years to come.

"Ah," you will say, "it's a great investment because real estate always appreciates." Well, like any other investment, it doesn't always appreciate, but that is really beside the point. Your first piece of real estate, your home, is not an investment, but a use asset. You need to use it. You aren't really paying rent, but you're paying lots of money to your mortgage company.

Your second piece of real estate is an investment. That's the one that you don't have to move out of and downsize to get at your equity. It's the one that you don't have to refinance and pay someone a lot more interest to get at your money. It's the one that, assuming that you rent it to someone, provides some cash flow to help defray some of the expenses required to own the property. But it's the one that you can sell or trade if you need some money.

The major downside, and we tend to forget this, is that real estate is not truly a liquid investment meaning that, unlike a security, sometimes it's very difficult to sell. You usually need a broker who'll take 3–6% off the top, closing costs, escrow companies, etc. I've always found that it's fun to speculate about the value of a piece of real estate. With securities, you can get current quotes every second of every day when markets are open, but with real estate, you can set your own values. "The house down the block sold for $2,000,000 two months ago, and my house must be worth at least that and probably more." You really have no idea what your house is worth until you try to sell it, and guessing its current value is really an exercise in fantasy.

"Ah," you will say, "I need the tax write-off." As you know, the mortgage interest you pay is tax deductible in most cases. With a good tax-deductible sum, you get some money back from the government when tax time rolls around. This makes you feel good, and it's an important tax break that benefits a lot of people and helps individuals purchase their own home, which generally keeps the economy humming along.

One of the funniest things that clients sometimes talk about is that their CPA, or tax guy, recommends that they take out a large mortgage on their house because they don't have enough tax deductions on their income tax return. This is a case of ignorant clients and stupid CPAs. It has never made a lot of sense to me to take out a larger mortgage just to get a tax deduction. You, of course, might have a very good reason to take out a mortgage, second mortgage, or an equity line of credit just in case, but to refinance just for a tax deduction, is really stupid. Let's see!

Let's assume that you have $10,000 in mortgage interest. For most people, you can deduct that, which means you can save about $3,500 in taxes. So let's take a hard look at this transaction. I borrow money. I pay interest. I get a tax deduction. So let's see. I pay some bank $10,000 in interest, and I get to save $3,500 in taxes. I've actually paid out of pocket almost three times the money I saved. I'm out of pocket, after it's all said and done, about $6,500. Gosh, I spent 3 to get 1. Does that make any sense? You, as a smart client, certainly will see through that plan. It amazes me how many people don't see it that way.

The other thing I want to emphasize is that no matter what your house is worth, in order to get real money, i.e., long green, is to borrow it out and pay someone interest to have it, or sell your house and downsize. A lot of people are selling their homes in California, for example, and moving to Cumquat, Idaho; Nevada; Arizona; or New Mexico where you can buy about twice the house for half the money.

A house and a home are good investments, but like everything else, you have to be aware of the pitfalls, total costs, and the reality of owning property.

Children

Don't you love the little darlings? They are so sweet and cuddly, and as my wife says, it's really a good thing they're so cute because sometimes you feel like . . . Well, children are a wonderful and expensive part of a person's lifetime. Most people have them because they want kids, but almost nobody has a clue about what a kid is going to cost them before they're launched, leave the nest, and begin taking care of themselves.

It's instructive to have some idea about what a kiddo is going to cost you because you have to factor a child into your calculations if you want to be rich.

Just for the fun of it, let's think about some of the expenses. Do you have an idea of how much you're going to spend on diapers, toys, clothes, sleepers, cribs, car seats, and photos? That's just the first couple of years.

Then, we go on to soccer games, electronic toys, batteries, day care (about $5,000 a year), bicycles, books, TV, tapes, holiday gifts, reindeer food, high chairs, and whatever else you can imagine.

Then, there are dentists, private school, special lessons, piano, ballet, karate classes, gas, and gray hair just getting them to and from whatever they're doing. Ah, let's not forget the orthodontist who is going to give them the million-dollar smile.

Then, there are shots, doctor visits, health insurance, trips, more clothes and toys to keep up with the other kids. Peer pressure is big here.

Then, there are more—private school, or if you're lucky, public school, cars, and more expensive toys.

Let's not forget college and everything that means.

Anyway, over the first twenty-two years of a child's life, you are probably going to spend somewhere north of $250,000 to prepare the little darling for a lifetime of bliss.

So, you see, it is a substantial chunk of dough that you are going to have to have in addition to the money you are trying to put away in your own account that is going to make you rich. The point is, you have to be even more intentional about saving and investing if you're going to get to your goals.

XXVI

Insurance

The problem with insurance is that when you really need it, you can't have it. If you don't have insurance and you get in a car wreck, you can't go out and buy it later just because you need it. If you don't have life insurance and you come down with some sort of cancer, you're not going to be able to buy it. Therefore, you're going to have to be like a lot of people who hate paying premiums and bite the bullet and buy protection for your family.

If you're young and have kids and mortgages, you also should have insurance. I don't recommend whole life for young people because the premiums are expensive, and you are in the accumulation phase of your life, but if you happen to get on the wrong plane, you should provide protection for your spouse and kids by having adequate term insurance.

You're probably thinking that since you're a woman, you don't need insurance. But let me set you straight. If you're a working woman with children, how is your spouse or partner going to make up the costs of losing your salary and continue caring for the children without your help and participation? Kids are expensive, and a woman should have insurance just as a man should have. Let's say you earn $50,000. If you should die, how is your husband going to survive without your salary or daily help? He's going to have to pay for a nanny or super day care because he's going to have to take care of the kids without you. Do a simple calculation, and figure that with a 6% return on the proceeds of a life insurance policy, you're going to need north of $800,000 to replace your salary of $50,000. You should buy a twenty-year term policy for about that amount.

In other words, both parents should have policies. How many do? Damn few. Stuff does happen. As has been said, life is what happens to you while you're making plans.

Insurance is the one thing you really need to have because if you don't have it, you can't get it when and if you really need it.

XXVII

College Planning

As I've said before, kids are expensive. Putting kids through four years of college, whether public or private, can cost a lot of money. In 2015, a private school probably will cost you about $60,000 a year when it's all said and done. So how, in addition to all the other things you should be doing, do you put money away for the university? Unless Jane or Johnny is extremely bright or athletic and get a full ride, you had better have some money put away.

Yes, you might get a scholarship or a student loan, but at some point, you have to pay the piper. There are a couple of tools you can use now that weren't available in years gone by, and you should take advantage of them. The 529 plans are a good place to start, but like the other ways to save money, you should start early, like when the baby is one year old, and you should put a nice chunk of money into a good plan. With any luck, God willing and the creek don't rise, you'll have enough money when your child is eighteen, to put them through four years of college.

Another good way to fund college is to put $10–12,000 a year away for four or five years in zero-coupon tax-free municipals that can grow into a substantial sum over fifteen to eighteen years.

A trap that I've noticed over the years is the custodian account. Parents used to put money into a custodian account for little Janey and plan that the kid uses it for college. But what happens if at age eighteen, the cute little kid joins the circus, hooks up with someone named "Biker," or begins to sniff it up their noses. Believe me, this happens more often than we'd care to think about. With a custodian account, when the child gets to be eighteen, that money legally belongs to her. You can't do a darn thing about it. That kid can cash it all in and use it for anything she'd like to do with it.

More and more parents are simply earmarking funds for college and leaving the registration in their personal names. 529 plans avoid the trap described above, and it points out, once again, how important registration of an account is.

Let's take a moment and talk about investments that are appropriate for funding a kid's college education. As a smart broker, I like two kinds: (1) zero-coupon bonds and (2) 529 plans.

If you start early enough, you can fund a college education by using the multiplying power of US Treasury bonds. These are bonds that you buy at their present value, and then when they mature at a year that you pick, you have their full face value. This can be also done using tax-free municipals, and it is up to you to determine which you prefer. For example, if you are going to need $25,000 a year for college, you are going to need about $100,000 face value of bonds. You can set this up so that you have $25,000 maturing each year during the child's university career. In 2015, interest rates are so low that you need to put more money aside, but the theory still works.

It used to be that your numbers would look something like this:

Assuming the child is just born, and you have a need for $25,000 each year when baby reaches 18, 19, 20, and 21, you could fund this by buying the following zero-coupon bonds:

For $25,000 of 18-year bonds, you'd need $15,000.
For $25,000 of 19-year bonds, you'd need $14,850.
For $25,000 of 20-year bonds, you'd need $14,525.
For $25,000 of 21-year bonds, you'd need $ 14,000.

To sum up, as of 2015, you could fund $100,000 worth of a university education for just a little under $58,400. You would have peace of mind and the assurance that the money would be there for your little darling. Obviously, the price of these zeros change, but the maturity value will be there when you need it.

The other investment is called a 529 plan. This is a tax-deferred plan that you can put away in the name of your child, where the investment amounts are put into the securities markets. You can invest all the way from conservative to aggressive, and the choice is generally yours. Among the plusses of a 529 is the fact that they have age-appropriate investments. Depending on the age of the child, the kiddo will wind up with a more aggressive portfolio when he is young and a more conservative portfolio as the child reaches college age. The money is the child's, but if the kid doesn't turn out the way you want her to, you can use the money for other people's education.

Some people like the assurance of a guarantee, and others like the excitement of an investment account. I personally like the security of a guarantee because I can't predict where the market's going to be eighteen years from now.

There has been a huge change in the way parents invest money for their children in the years since I started out. In the early days, parents would set up a custodian account for little Johnny or Suzie. What happens, however, is that this money absolutely belongs to the children. So if at the age of eighteen, your little darling wants to buy a Harley and trip around, there is no way you can legally keep that money away from them. Therefore, a lot of parents have started simply earmarking the money and leaving it in their own accounts so that the kids have no access to it.

XXVIII

Retirement Planning

Good Money and Bad Money

An important corollary to total financial planning is to realize that there are basically two kinds of money: good money and bad money. You will quickly say that all money is good money, and I must admit that having money is better than having none, but I want you, as a smart client, to realize that money, when invested, is put into different kinds of pots or buckets. These pots are known by various names such as IRAs, tax-free bonds, stocks, mutual funds, taxable bonds, 401(k)s, annuities, limited partnerships, and almost anything else that Wall Street thinks will sell.

I have a general rule. If you put money into an investment that is hard to get out of—read convertible to usable cash—without a tax penalty or income tax, it is bad money.

If you put money into an investment that is easy to convert into usable cash, it is good money.

For example, if you have $100,000 in an IRA, and you wish to convert into cash, you, if you're not 59½, will generally pay a 10% tax penalty plus your regular income tax, which will usually amount to about 40% of the $100,000. In other words, you will pay about $50,000 to withdraw your $100,000 from your IRA. It doesn't make a lot of sense to reduce your capital by 50% to get at your money.

Therefore, I think that money in an IRA or other qualified plan or annuity is bad money.

That makes it important to not only put money away for retirement, but to put money into regular old taxable accounts that can be used to buy houses, cars, trips, clothes, etc. Remember the analogy about fighting a war? Hopefully, with these examples, you can see why there is "good money" and "bad money." So it becomes very important, while you're planning ahead, to make sure that you have money that grows on a tax-deferred basis and money that grows on a currently taxable basis.

XXIX

Stocks, Bonds, and Mutual Funds

Now we're going to have a quick overview of different types of investments. When I started in the business five decades ago, there were basically three forms of investments: stocks, bonds, and mutual funds. These still form the backbone of almost everything you can do, but the difference today is that there are hundreds, if not thousands, of variations these can now take.

Stocks, or equities, are the basic building blocks of a person's portfolio. A share of stock represents ownership in a company or business. A smart broker will tell you that you are not just buying a share of stock, but you are actually buying into an ongoing and hopefully a growing business. This means that you are participating in a capitalist system of free enterprise. The object of investing is to make money, and we've talked before about the pitfalls and mistakes people make. I think that among the worst things that can happen to you as a new investor is to watch your first purchase appreciate significantly in value. This misleads you into thinking that making money in the market is easy. Remember, if it were easy, we'd all be on that fabled beach in Tahiti.

Another bad thing that can happen to you is if you turn out to be a "one-shot wonder." I can't tell you how many stupid clients begin their investing career by getting two or three thousand dollars together and then buying something that they heard about from some "expert" brother-in-law who "really follows the market." First of all, it's really dumb to buy something from a brother-in-law expert who "really follows the market." Secondly, it's really dumb to think that your $3,000 will ever grow into a meaningful sum. Remember the rule of 72. At 10% a year, it would take you about 60 years to get to a million dollars. That's too long to wait. Don't be a one-shot wonder! You need to invest $3,000 every six months or so in good-quality stocks to have anything worthwhile while you're still able to enjoy it.

Remember, equities have returned, depending on how you define it, an average of about 10% a year for 100 years. Clearly, this hasn't happened in a straight line, and some years you've got to wonder what you're doing in the market, but it's still the best way to accumulate wealth that we have. Remember, when the market is way down, you should buy!

Far better than buying one stock on a "hunch, let's go to lunch, get a hunch and buy a bunch" type of philosophy is putting your money into a mutual fund that has a good long-term track record of superior returns.

Before we talk about mutual funds, let's talk about a category of security that is almost completely overlooked by brokers and individuals. It is a fact that the richer you are, the more money you have in bonds. In many large brokerage firms, the biggest and most experienced brokers have 50–60% of all the assets under their control invested in bonds. Why? Because they're generally safe, and rich people generally like safety. It's true that rich people have a mix of stocks and bonds, but they will have a large percentage of their assets in safer fixed-income securities, or bonds.

A broker friend of mine used to train rookie brokers, and he used to lecture them on the importance of bonds. A number of them wanted to be gunslingers and buy nothing but aggressive stocks. One day, one of them griped that my friend was old enough to be his father. My friend, without missing a beat, said, "Maybe I am. What was your mother's name?"

When I was a rookie broker, the stock market was so bad that nobody wanted to talk about stocks. And yes, I was one of those people who called you up and wanted you to buy securities from me. For the first three years in the business, I made 50 phone contacts a day, 5 days a week. That was the key to success in those days. The numbers were as follows: 100 phone contacts, 15 prospects, and 3 accounts.

Anyway, back to the story. The market was so bad that if I mentioned I was a stockbroker, I'd usually get a response that you can't print in a family paper, or I'd get a "not interested" and a hang up. So I changed my approach. I would call people up and ask them "if they were interested in getting some tax-free income from their investments?" In those days, the marginal tax rate was 70%, which means if you got 10% on your taxable savings, you'd have to pay 70% of it to the government in the form of taxes, and you would only net 3%. So there were a lot of people interested in hearing my story.

There are many kinds of bonds, but you can generally group them into two types: taxable and nontaxable. It's true that income from US Treasuries are tax-free in your state, but they are taxable by the federal government, so you have to give back 30–35% of your income. With regular old corporate bonds, certificates of deposit, and other securities that are fully taxable, you have to pay federal tax and state tax, so you have to give back about 40–45% of your income. If you're not making any money, your tax bracket might be lower, and you may not have to pay quite so much, but we're talking about the average investor. Anyway, I love not paying taxes. *Tax evasion* is bad and will get you some time in the slam. *Tax avoidance* is good and will put more money in your pocket. So let's talk about tax-free or municipal bonds. There are hundreds of municipal bonds because every town, city, county, state, water district, school district, municipal utility company, some ball parks (although these are different and a little less desirable), redevelopment agencies, roads, highways, sewage treatment plants, power plants, and almost anything else a governmental entity that's not the federal government one can imagine needs lots of money, and there is no easier way than to borrow it.

And the beauty of these bonds is that the income from them is totally tax-free. You pay no federal tax and no state tax if the bonds are from your state of residence. That's where the concept of tax equivalent yield comes into play. For example, if you are able to get 5% today on a tax-free security, it is equivalent to getting roughly 8% on a taxable security, and you can't get 8% on a taxable security with a similar degree of safety of principal and interest. Furthermore, you can get insured municipal bonds, which means that if for some reason your bond would default (quit paying interest or principal), an insurance company would pay off full principal and interest. After the panic of 2008, this has become harder.

It would be misleading to not talk about how bonds fluctuate in market value. Bonds will continue to pay interest, but the market value will change with interest rates. If interest rates go up, existing bonds will go down in value. The income will be the same, but you'll wake up and look at your statement and wonder where the principal went. The reasons are simple, but beyond the scope of this explanation. If you hold the bonds to maturity, you'll get your complete principal. By the way, bonds are almost always sold in multiples of $1,000. The other risk is the creditworthiness of the issuing authority.

As I said, rich people like safety and income, and I haven't bought an uninsured municipal bonds in fifteen years. Insured municipals are always rated AAA, the highest rating possible. Ratings can go from AAA to BBB, and there are several gradations in between. Anything lower than BBB is really considered junk. Save your money, and don't buy them even though you are tempted by the higher rates that they pay. As I have said, after 2008, this has changed.

There are more mutual funds in the world than there are stocks listed on all the different exchanges. In a previous chapter, we talked about how some magazines are always touting last year's hot funds and how stupid that usually is, so the question becomes, how do you pick a good mutual fund? The answer is not so easy to define. I think that the only way you can protect yourself is to find a good broker to help you evaluate funds that fit your investment objectives. Look at the expense ratio, the commissions you have to pay, the management fees, and the track record of the fund. It's very hard to tell, for example, if the people who manage a fund and who have a good track record stay with the fund. They often move around quite a bit as other funds are always trying to buy them away from where they are. These changes affect the way the fund is managed, and you usually you can't find out about any changes within any meaningful time frame.

There are also exchange-traded funds and index funds available that some studies say outperform money managers. Give them a look.

Another problem with funds is that success often breeds future failure. Because a successful fund is usually touted by the media, stupid people send lots of money to the fund. As a fund receives buckets full of money, it has to put the money to work. As they put it to work, they have to seek out and buy stocks that are more and more marginal. As they get more of these kinds of stocks, they begin to lose performance, and the fund begins to fall behind its past performance. That's why funds don't always perform in the future as they have performed in the past.

Therefore, stick with the tried and true. Go with funds that have good long-term records and that have been through the wars.

An even better option is to employ professional money managers. Today, most brokerage firms have a number of very good money managers available to their clients, sometimes for as little as $50,000. This allows you to tailor your portfolios with the proper asset allocation to dovetail with your risk tolerance. You can judge your performance compared to certain benchmarks and find out if you are outperforming or underperforming the markets. If you are underperforming, you can change your manager just like you change your shirts.

The best part is that these managers are price competitive with mutual funds and in some cases are cheaper. Another huge advantage is that you can find out immediately if there are any changes in the individuals who actually manage portfolio. The brokerage firms, as part of their due diligence, watch their stable of managers very closely and will cull the bad ones very quickly.

Masters of the Universe

If you really want to get a feel for how Wall Street works and what the really big guys do, you should read *Bonfire of the Vanities* by Tom Wolfe and *Liar's Poker* by Michael Lewis. Both of them accurately portray a lot of the shenanigans that take place on Wall Street and how easy it is sometimes for people to make a lot of money when you put crafty brokers together with stupid clients.

It's hard for a retail broker, meaning a broker who deals with the general public, to make a *lot* of money because the general public doesn't have a *lot* of money. A good, honest retail broker can make a very comfortable living and in reality can accumulate a great deal of money, but to make the really big money as a broker or advisor, you have to go to the places where a great deal of money changes hands, and that's usually where the institutions live. Both of these books are good reads and can do a lot to help you see how cutthroat Wall Street can be and why the average person needs a good, honest retail broker. I said it before, "Wall Street is a jungle, and to deal with it, you need a good jungle guide." Your broker can help you do that.

That's another reason I detest some of these misleading commercials for cheap brokers that you see in the media. You get what you pay for, and you ain't getting much if you deal with some schmuck. Furthermore, the old saying about the attorney who represents himself in court who has a fool for a client is true. If you, with some rare exceptions, think you can do it yourself, you are just another stupid client.

XXXI

The Really Big Guys

Everything needs to be put into perspective. What is rich? How much money does a person need? Usually, the answer is, "If I just had $1,000,000 more than I have right now."

Can money buy happiness? No, but it can help. As it is said, "I've been poor and I've been rich. Rich is better."

Unfortunately, about 60% of everyone retires with about a net worth of $70,000 and an income only a little bit above social security. That means that excluding their house, they have almost no real money in case of emergency. It means that if it weren't for Medicare, they'd be like life was back in the first half of the last century.

There wouldn't be much. There still isn't much for these folks. If you get out of the upscale suburbs and drive around the country a bit, you'll see for yourself that people don't live in many fancy houses. That's why mobile-home parks are so popular. They're cheap and usually affordable.

I do think, however, that living in a mobile-home park is like a form of feudalism. Usually, you don't own your pad, you have no control over your rent, and you can't really move because other parks don't want your mobile home. In fact, I'd go so far as to call residents of most mobile-home parks chattel slaves. Maybe this is a good reason to accumulate enough money to live somewhere else during retirement.

STUPID BROKERS, STUPID CLIENTS

I always joke with my wife about living our golden years in a doublewide in Nevada. She doesn't think this is funny, but it sure is a way to live cheaply.

So how much is rich? To the person barely scraping by, a million bucks seems like rich. To the person who has one million dollars, it seems like two or three millions dollars is rich. To the person who has five million dollars, ten seems like it would be rich. To be rich, you can't be able to count your money. You need to have enough to live like people live on that television show. You need your own jet, your own home on the Riviera, your own bodyguards, and enough capital that produces enough income that you can't possibly spend it.

Then come the problems of managing it. What do you do with it? How do you make sure people like you and not just your money? How many sycophants do you need to adequately keep your butt smooched? My dad used to say that "as long as you pour the booze, you'll have a houseful of friends." After sixty years, I have learned that he's right.

How do you know you can trust your accountants and money managers? How do you know you're getting the best advice? How do you keep track of it all? Doesn't it make you crazy or a little paranoid? How about the fear of losing it all? Remember during the great crash in 1929, people jumped out of buildings because they were wiped out and couldn't stand the thought of having nothing? Some people killed their entire families because they couldn't stand the thought of not being able to continue to care for them in the way they were accustomed. Yes, having money is good, but it can be a huge trap, and there is no easy out. Having money is still better than not having it, but you have to learn to deal with it. Some people never do.

There are shrinks who specialize in helping people deal with not having any money, and there are shrinks who help people with lots of money and how to deal with their fear of losing it. Money isn't easy. It is the curse of many smart brokers, especially when they're starting out, of having to deal with very rich people, and sometimes that causes severe psychological problems of inferiority. If a smart broker is also a good broker, that broker will accumulate money, and one day, having five or ten million dollars won't seem like such a big deal.

Of course, it helps if you're a smart broker who starts out coming from a rich background. Then, the problem is reversed. These kind of brokers have never had to work for a living and find that money management is easy because they're used to managing their own. Then, the problem is different. These brokers have great disdain for people who are starting out poor. Money is its own conundrum and has its own problems. You have to learn to deal with that.

But back to the big guys. They equate having vast amounts of money with their own infallibility. The Greeks had it right, hubris brings its own fate or downfall. As the Bible says, "Pride goeth before the fall." Thus, you have the stories of Enron, WorldCom, Madoff, Tyco, and countless others. They thought they could do no wrong, but they got caught.

One of my not so pet peeves is how large golden parachutes are. In case you've been living in a cave, a golden parachute is the monetary handshake between companies and former executives when they either voluntarily or involuntarily leave their executive posts. Usually, these dollar gifts amount to tens of millions of dollars and sometimes amount to hundreds of millions. I think this is obscene and borders on the criminal. How many executives have really run their companies into the ground and then parted with huge sums of money? Maybe they know where all the bodies are buried, and the people who stay behind are afraid of what they know. Actually, I think the people on the board who vote for these hope one day they'll get the same. I don't have the answer, but there ought to be a law.

XXXII

Estate Taxes

If you're the kind of person who has decided to work all your life and accumulate a reasonably sized estate and then when you shuffle off this mortal coil, you want to give a large percentage of most everything you have to the government, you can skip this chapter, or better yet, you can leave your estate to me and my children.

Actually, the percent of your estate that is taxed away by the government is in serious flux. Congress, in its wisdom, decided to change the amount of your estate that is free from taxes almost every year until 2010 when the estate tax disappeared for the whole year. So if you were planning to die, your best bet would be to have planned to die in 2010. If you miscalculate and live until 2011, the old rates and exemptions applied, and you would have been able to only be able to pass along to your beneficiaries $650,000 before the residual of your estate is taxed at 55%. Does this make any sense? No, but then, does Congress ever make much sense?

Actually, it's more complicated than what I've described above, and it's an important thing to have a competent and capable estate attorney do the planning for you. This individual will write a good document, probably a living trust, to maximize the amount you can pass on to your heirs or favorite charities and minimize the amount of tax that your accommodating federal and state government will steal from your family.

In 2015, the amount that can pass free is $5,000,000, but the government can change that anytime.

Remember, I've said that if you don't plan and write the right kind of document, your friendly state will provide you with a will that will distribute your money as they see fit and probably not as you would want. So do it!

A corollary problem is that maybe your parents have an estate problem and may not even realize how bad their problem is. I believe it is your responsibility to talk with them as best you can. This is often a very difficult thing to do, but unless you want to see a lot of your rightful inheritance get hijacked by the government, you should do this. A good way to do it is to take them to an estate planning seminar where they usually talk about how much estates are minimized by taxes and costs. Sometimes, they will have the exact numbers from some famous people who failed to plan and then had their assets and taxes spread all over the public airways because they only had a will that needed probate, and remember, a will is a public document. A living trust is not, and your estate will not be made public.

You may remember comments made by Bill Gates and Warren Buffet when they said that the estate tax should not be repealed, and it's only fair to give money to the government when you die. Well, I suppose that when you have billions of dollars, you might not miss a couple of billion here or there. I mean, how many billions do you really need? Don't you lose count after a while? Well, I think they're wrong. Most of us don't have billions and would rather keep what we have in the family, thank you. Lately, there has been a movement by billionaires to give half of their wealth to charity. They usually give it to a personal-estate tax-deductible family charity and then hire their kids to run it.

The numbers and percentages I've mentioned above only really apply to what I've called good money. Bad money, or IRAs and other qualified plans, can be taxed away at the rates above plus ordinary income tax rates. So you could see your parents' $1,000,000 IRA get hit with a total tax of close to $800,000. Pretty ugly, isn't it?

Insurance is another matter. If you have a large policy and you own it, it will pay off to your heirs at your death, and they won't pay any income tax on it, but they will have to count it as part of your estate for estate tax purposes. There are ways to prevent this, such as an irrevocable life insurance trust that takes the ownership out of your personal estate, and upon your death, the proceeds will pass income and estate tax-free to your heirs. Some people have their beneficiaries actually own the trust, and as long as they pay the premiums, it'll be out of your estate. For my feeble brain, the insurance trust is a better solution because I find it's a simpler concept. You will need a good estate attorney to write it up for you.

There is a very cool option that takes paying estate taxes completely out of the equation. It's called the zero tax option. I think it's very slick, and it works like this: let's say you have some favorite charities, or you want to endow a professorship or a scholarship at your favorite university. Let's say you have a north of $5,000,000 estate. Instead of paying the government some meaningful percentage of that money, you plan to give the money to your favorite charities. Gifts to charities are not taxed by the government and escape the death tax. You then write an insurance trust and fund it with a $5,000,000 insurance policy. Depending on your age and the type of insurance, it may cost you $50–60,000 a year in premiums, but when you die, your heirs will get the $5,000,000 free of taxes. So in this case, your charities are very happy and name stuff after you, and your kids get all the money. The government gets zip. Yes!

By the way, I think whole life insurance is a better way to fund a trust rather than term because with term, you may have a low-level premium for twenty years or so, but if you should happen to live for twenty-years plus one day, you could see your annual premium jump from maybe $7,000 for a $1,000,000 policy to something approaching $200,000 a year. Now you're not going to pay that much money unless you have a terminal illness and know you're going to croak in a short time, so you'll let the policy lapse. With whole life, the premiums stay low forever or vanish entirely.

The problem is that when you really need insurance, you can't get it, and you can't get the cheap kind under any circumstances. You have to do all of this when you're healthy and happy. If you've got serious health problems, you can't do this at all, and the option is closed to you.

Insurance and trusts are extremely complicated There are Charitable Remainder Trust, Unitrusts, and others of all kinds. A good estate attorney will tailor your plan to fit your personal needs and objectives. Be sure to find a good estate attorney.

XXXIII

Nuts and Bolts

Paperwork
Living Trusts
Wills
Beneficiaries

We've already touched a bit on the necessity of keeping your paperwork up to date, but it's worth repeating again: what happens to your money after you pass is largely governed by the paperwork that you have.

You'll remember the story of Sam who neglected to put his new wife's name on the beneficiary form for his IRA, and his ex-wife from hell inherited the whole thing, and his new wife got Zippo. Changing the beneficiary as your situations change is a fairly simple thing to do, but unless it's taken care of, it can turn into an absolute disaster.

A will is also a simple thing to do, and it's surprising how many people die intestate, which is a legal term for dying without a will. But don't worry, as we've said, your friendly state government has one already prepared for you. The state will appoint an administrator who will charge an arm and a leg for overseeing the process of distributing your assets according to the laws of that particular state. The problem with this is that your money can wind up going to places that you would never want it to go. Long-lost relatives can show up and put in a claim, and you'd roll over in your grave if you knew about some of the people that can get your money. Don't be lulled into believing that your spouse will get it all as the laws are fickle, and absent a will or trust, your money will not always go where you want it to.

There is another problem with wills. In the old days, when life was simpler, it was common for folks to write a simple will that basically said, "When husband dies, wife gets it, and if wife dies first, then husband gets it." Then, when the last spouse dies, the kids get it. The problem with this is that a will must be probated. This is generally not a problem at the first death, but can be very expensive at the second death. Typically, an attorney is needed to get the will to and through the courts, and for that bit of work, the attorney will generally get about 3–5% of the estate. Then, there is the executor of the estate, and sometimes, but not usually, this person will take another 5% bite of the apple.

Furthermore, it is a slow and public process. If you want all your neighbors to know what you're leaving to whom, write a will.

One other major problem with a will is what happens to you if you get incapacitated like if you have a stroke or get Alzheimer's. This means that you can't manage your affairs by yourself, and although some people will try to get around it by giving someone a power of attorney, generally, you will need a conservatorship, which means that a court and judge will appoint someone to oversee your affairs, pay your bills, dispose of your property, and rip off your estate for some more money. The conservator may not even be someone whom you would ordinarily trust to do things right by you and in fact might be a total stranger.

There is no perfect solution, but I like people to have a living trust. A living trust is created and, at first glance, appears to be a pretty wordy document, but believe me, each word is important. You can still control your property, name a successor trustee to take care of you in the event of your incapacitation, avoid probate, and control who gets what, make provisions for your spouse, and if you're married, pass along twice as much property to your heirs without estate tax as you can with a simple will. You should have a good attorney write it up for you as the laws do change. You should review it every couple of years.

I mentioned "trust mills" before, and I'll mention them again. They are traps, and if you have any assets at all, you shouldn't be afraid of spending a few additional bucks to protect your estate from unscrupulous people and a greedy government.

An important point to remember is that after you're gone, stuff happens. Beneficiaries begin to feel cheated, left out, and ignored. "Why, I did so much for him, a lot more than my brother did, and he got most of the money!" So the big litigation battle begins. Sometimes, it's smart to have your attorney videotape your statement showing that you are of sound mind and body and are taking these decisions seriously and without any form of coercion or duress.

Another big thing about paperwork is knowing where it is. Sometimes, the paperwork is not in obvious places. You should let your spouse or someone else know where the important papers are. This means that you must be organized. I'm lucky in that my wife is very organized and generally knows where the stuff is. What I have to be careful of is making sure that I give the paperwork to her and that she knows what it is. Over the years, I'm not being sexist here, but I find that women tend to be uninformed when it comes to money matters. This can be a huge problem. It's not because they are unable, but it's because many men assume the role of handling the money and investments in the household. The men pay the taxes, make the investment decisions, open and maintain accounts, and the result is that the wife, when the husband dies, has no clue about investments and finds herself afloat among the flotsam and jetsam of a lifetime of money and investing. In fact, I have, over the years, given many seminars to women just to educate them in what they should know. Women must be educated about money and must be partners with the men in their lives.

They should know where and why the family is doing things. They should read assiduously and become informed about different kinds of investments. They should not just sign the income tax forms, but should review them and be aware of where all the money comes from and where it goes.

In fact, and here I add it parenthetically, when a parent dies, and you have to sort out the finances of the deceased person, a great place to start is with last year's income tax forms. This will provide you with a list of everyplace that sent a tax reporting form to your decedent. This will enable you to find out where your parent squirreled away money. Many times, especially in the elderly, you will find that there may be a dozen accounts holding various sums of money, accounts they never mentioned to you, and if you don't find them, they will eventually be escheated to the state, and after a time, the state gets to keep the money.

Sometimes it's a good idea to just check the website of your secretary of state to see if there is any money under your name. It's interesting what you can find and sometimes very profitable. You can find estate money, forgotten funds, lost income tax refunds, and all sorts of free money.

XXXIV

Time Lines for Becoming a Millionaire

or
How Long Does It Take?

Some of the most common questions that I'm asked have to do with "How'm I doing?" "Am I on track?" "How much money will I have when I retire?" "Will I have enough to retire on?" I know we've dealt with this before, but that was mostly in a theoretical way, generally starting when people are young and have their whole future ahead of them.

More pertinent, however, is what the numbers are like for people who are 25, 30, 35, 40, 45, or even 50? Therefore, I'm going to make a few assumptions about rates of return, age, and contribution amounts that you need in order to reach a goal of $1,500,000 by the time you are 65. Obviously, there are a whole lot of variables, and it's really necessary to run the numbers every year or so to see how you're tracking. Market returns vary greatly, and you should contribute enough to continue to be on the right track. For this purpose, I'm going to use the historic stock market return of 10% per year, but as you know, because you are now a smart client, rates of return vary. The most dangerous trap is to assume that markets will always go the same way, whether up or down. During the boom of the late '90s, I could just picture all the Silicon Valley dot-comers sitting in front of their computers, doing a straight-line extrapolation on their Excel programs and thinking they're always going to be fine. So use this table with care. It's helpful, but you need to use it as a guide, for it's also true that for any given number of assumptions, there are many different combinations of outcomes.

TABLE

Age	Rate of Return	Goal at 65	Contributions Per Year
25	10%	$1,500,000	$3,400
30	10%	$1,500,000	$5,535
35	10%	$1,500,000	$9,118
40	10%	$1,500,000	$15,250
45	10%	$1,500,000	$26,200
50	10%	$1,500,000	$47,200

See! It's not so hard.

As we've talked about before, the earlier you start, the better and more likely it is that you're going to reach your goal. A couple of caveats: you should make sure you're saving to your good-money taxable account as well as your bad money tax-deferred account.

Good luck and good investing!

Remember, when someone says it isn't about the money, it's always about the money.

About the Author

The author draws on his extensive and successful experience on Wall Street from the vantage point of five decades in the brokerage business. The author was a certified financial planner and has been candid about his knowledge and history. This book will reveal the inner workings and development of a career over almost fifty years.

The names of everyone mentioned in the book are changed, and any relationship to persons living or dead is purely coincidental. The events, however, are factual. Investment, retirement and insurance strategies are believed to be accurate at the time of this writing. If you try to pursue any of them, you must obtain proper legal advice as laws and rules governing investment strategies do change.

www.ingramcontent.com/pod-product-compliance
Lightning Source LLC
Chambersburg PA
CBHW030837180526
45163CB00004B/1363